Prayer, Stress, and Our Inner Wounds

Prayer, Stress, and Our Inner Wounds

Flora Slosson Wuellner

THE UPPER ROOM

Nashville, Tennessee

Scripture quotations not otherwise identified are from the Revised Standard
Version of the Bible, copyrighted 1946, 1952, and © 1971 by the Division of
Christian Education, National Council of the Churches of Christ in the United
States of America, and are used by permission.

Scripture passages designated TEV are from the *Good News Bible, The Bible in
Today's English Version,* copyright by the American Bible Society 1966, 1971, ©
1976, and are used by permission.

Book and Cover Design: Harriette Bateman
First Printing: March, 1985 (5)
Second Printing: September, 1985 (3)
Third Printing: March, 1986 (5)
Library of Congress Catalog Card Number: 84-051830
ISBN 0-8358-0501-8
Printed in the United States of America

This book
is lovingly dedicated
to our daughters:
Christine, Virginia, and Lucy

CONTENTS

INTRODUCTION

This book has been growing as long as I have been growing. As a young girl, when I first read the life of Jesus in the Gospels, I thought: *If God is really like* that, *we are in safe hands!*

What do we see in the face and the acts of Jesus that tells us about God? We see the transforming power of healing on all possible levels: body, emotions, memories, relationships, decisions, purpose. We see transforming healing in individuals and in groups. And we see that the divine passion and compassion has never ended but flows toward us as a limitless, mighty stream.

During my years as parish pastor, and then as pastor in a specialized ministry of prayer, I have often met men and women who longed for deeper spiritual experience and radiant living but who were unaware of the inner blocks and unhealed inner wounds in themselves and in their families and communities.

Observing myself as well as others, I began to realize that there is a deep connection between our inner healing and our growing, healthy life of prayer and relationship. I began to realize that Jesus' passion for healing was a tremendous aspect of his ministry and that this ministry is still his life and the center of his relationship with us. I began to realize that we have laid far too much stress on concern for sin rather than concern for inner wounds and that we have depended on good resolutions and willpower rather than on the healing, transforming touch of God.

This book on our inner healing and transformation

combines explanation, examples, scripture references, and imagery prayer. It can be used by individuals, church groups, and families. The suggested alternative forms of guided imagery prayer can be especially helpful in a group setting because often we need the reassuring and nurturing presence of others while moving through painful areas of memory. Shared thoughts and experiences stimulate a growing mutual trust. However, it is important in a group setting never to urge or to require confidences. There are always some persons who, though needing the acceptance of a group, need to keep their memories, inner images, and experiences private, and they must feel free to do so.

I suggest that the individual or group first read through the whole book to get a clear idea of its approach and then reread more slowly for a deeper and more personal experience. It is best to move slowly through these areas of healing, returning if necessary to chapters that center around some special need.

There are many channels of God's healing in this world: good friends, families, pastors, counselors, doctors, psychologists, trained therapists, sharing groups. This book, with its suggested forms of healing prayer, is *not* meant to take the place of any necessary medical or psychological therapy; it is meant to augment, companion, and enrich the other channels of help if they are needed in times of special stress.

Nor is this book meant to take the place of the healing ministry of the church. In all my writing, my workshops, and my counseling, I urge any person moving toward inner emotional healing and deepening spiritual experience to become part of some church community. The family of God provides a nurturing context and a deep-rootedness, and it encourages a healthful responsibility of relationship. It is also a vital and compassionate channeling of God's healing to a world that is starving and agonizing for the transforming touch of love.

CHAPTER ONE

Our Hurting and Hungering

A picture that was hung in my room when I was a child changed my life. It was a picture of a shepherd climbing down a rugged cliffside; with one hand he gripped a rock and with the other he reached down to a sheep that had fallen to a ledge below. Its face looked up in terror and trust. A bird of prey circled overhead. I could not see the shepherd's face as he strained down to the sheep, but I could see the knotted muscles, the bleeding hands and arms gashed by thorns, the twisted garment torn in the steep descent.

"That's the Good Shepherd. That's Jesus," my parents told me.

I stared in amazement. This picture was very different from the one of the Good Shepherd on the wall of my Sunday school room. In that one a placid shepherd in a spotless white robe strolled along a grassy level path, carrying an equally spotless and placid lamb.

The shepherd in my picture was paying a real and painful price. I could see from the concentrated body and the compassionate authority of the outstretched hand that to reach the hurt and crying animal mattered more to him than anything else in the world. And I knew as I gazed at the picture that that sheep would be reached, held, healed, and lifted to life.

Through the years, God and the meaning of God came to me through that picture and changed me. Perhaps each of us can remember some such pivotal incident, some event, some book or picture or poem, some person, some experience of love or pain, that began to open to us something of the passion and compassion of God who enters our pain and stretches out healing hands forever.

God's love longs to touch and heal our inner wounds. God's transforming power can do it!

Sometimes it seems to me that now, more than ever before, we human beings are beginning to explore the exciting frontier of God's love. Perhaps more than ever before we are reaching out and experiencing the implications of the radical love of God through Jesus' presence in this world. I see this happening in spite of, perhaps *because* of, the pain and danger of the world around us.

I certainly see a change in the conscious awareness of church members I visit. I see a change in the hunger and longing of theological students. I see a change in pastors' groups I attend. I see a change in the wistful longing of many unchurched persons. I see a change in *me*.

A generation ago, churches of many different denominations were praying for a renewal of the power of the Holy Spirit. There were many startling results. Many of us felt the shaking of foundations as old walls, old structures came down. New forms of life, worship, language, communication, and service sprang up. Some of these manifestations seemed creative and renewing. Some of them were frightening and bewildering. We learned that it was only too easy to take the gifts of God and manipulate and distort them. Perhaps more was given to us than we could handle. Even so, today most of us find the Christian church a far more alive and exciting organism than it was a generation ago. The door is opened!

What is the Spirit doing among us now? There are many answers, for it is a many-sided glory. Recently, one answer came to me when I was talking with a ninety-year-old historian and politician whose mind is as alert as it ever was to the trends and ambiguities of the human scene.

"I am optimistic about the human race," he said to me, quietly smiling, while his gaze wandered over the hundreds of books on his shelves. "Yes, in spite of the problems and the dangers on every side, in many ways it is a better world

than it was when I was a boy in the 1890s. In spite of con-
tinuing wars, injustice, hatreds, nevertheless, this is probably the first century in the world's history in which so many
people in so many parts of the world have become so keenly
aware of the hurts and problems in other parts of the world.
Even though we may respond inadequately, this deepening,
expanding awareness has become part of our consciousness.
And I have seen many signs, especially in the last thirty
years, that compassionate concern is growing along with the
awareness." He smiled at me. "I think we're going to make
it!"

Awareness of pain as a manifestation of the Holy
Spirit? At first that startled me. But then I realized that the
Gospels make it clear that Jesus walked constantly in the
awareness of the pain of the world as well as in the
awareness of the beauty and potentiality of the world. He
shares with us the compassionate suffering of God as well as
the burning joy of God. A poignant word in scripture is that
of Matthew 9:35–36:

> Jesus went about all the cities and villages, teaching . . . and
> preaching . . . and healing . . . every infirmity. When he
> saw the crowds, he had compassion for them, because they
> were harassed and helpless like sheep without a shepherd.

The passion to heal was central in Jesus.

Of course the divine Spirit brings a new awareness of
pain. It is one of the mightiest of the signs. We see and
touch the suffering person, animal, maybe even the plant in
a new way and with a new sense of sharing because one of
the signs of the new spirit of compassion is awareness of our
own pain as well. This is another surprise for many of us.
We thought we would be made to forget our own inner
stress and suffering. We thought we would be lifted above it
as we immersed ourselves in concern and healing for others.
Not so. God's gift of sensitive, compassionate awareness,
slowly, painfully, circuitously growing in the human race
and in our hearts, must and will embrace every aspect of

this world's pain, including our own. Our ministry of caring must sooner or later touch the cries, the hurts, the hungers within. In the retreats and workshops I lead, I call these internal hurts our "wounded children." We should look on them with the same compassion and take them to the same healing hands as any other part of God's suffering creation.

For three years I served on a committee of my denomination that interviews pastors in order to hear and share their problems and explore ways of helping them through their difficulties. I was impressed by the hardworking, sacrificial quality of the lives of many of the pastors, but I also became aware of the unhealed wounds of the past and pain of the present that many of them were carrying around. I noticed that many of them were in a state of serious exhaustion. I also noticed that unlike many pastors in earlier generations, most of them felt that the pain and fatigue were *not* necessary and inevitable parts of the pastorate. Though they often did not know what to do about it, most of them believed that God wanted to do something about it. I have sensed a real change in the clergy. Increasingly, they are open to the importance and possibility of depth healing.

I have seen a change in many church members. Increasingly, the average Christian begins to realize that loving concern for the self is not the same as selfishness. Selfish people do not truly love their own selves. They may grasp compulsively, but that is often because they lack the inner nurturing that could open them freely to others. Still, it is not easy to learn to receive help.

In the thirteenth chapter of John, we see Jesus kneeling before his friends, taking their tired, dusty feet tenderly into his hands and washing them. Try to picture yourself there in that room with Jesus kneeling before you, offering his personal, loving service. What a shock! We are the ones who ought to be down on our knees serving. But he says to us, even as he said to Peter (with a humorous and understanding smile in his eyes, I'm sure), "If you don't let me do this for you, Peter, or _____ (here add your own name), you don't belong to me!"

Only *after* he had lovingly served and ministered to each one of them did he challenge and command them to reach out and lovingly minister to each other. He was not being just a role model of service to them. I believe he was bringing each of them the nurturing, healing touch, so that they, as healed persons, could be free to touch others lovingly.

How many of us are trying to "wash the feet" of others when we ourselves need help?

How fully, freely, and wholly can we reach out to others when we ourselves are inwardly broken and hungry?

Do we really believe that God does not infinitely care that we, friends, disciples, servants, are hurting and needing the healing touch?

The first step for transforming this world's pain is to look with honesty at our own pain and to begin to open this door to God's love. We often speak of sin in our church services. Always there is a place in our liturgies for private or communal confession of sin and the receiving of forgiveness. But very seldom is there a place in our liturgies for the expression of our wounds. The sin and the wound are not the same thing. We need both forgiveness and healing, or we do not become whole persons. God is equally concerned with both.

One way I have learned to distinguish between a sin that is to be forgiven and a wound that is to be healed is the way I feel after inner confession. When I have been confronting a sin, an act or decision of hurtfulness made in freedom of choice, I feel a sharp but releasing pain, like the lancing of an abscess. When I am confronting and trying to confess a wound, an act rising out of fear, phobia, pain, or unhealed memory, I feel no sharp sense of relief, and a dull pain continues to throb. Then I know that the problem is not sin needing to be forgiven but a genuine inner wound needing the touch of the Divine Physician.

This realization removes an enormous burden of guilt

and heaviness. We must try to help one another, both in our relationships and in our church services, to distinguish more clearly between our sins, acts done in freedom, and our wounds, acts rising out of *un*freedom. For God deals with them differently, and different forms of prayer are needed.

Stressful living is life in a state of prolonged, unhealed woundedness and unfed hunger. Obviously we all have occasional times of stress, but this does not become stressful living unless we ignore the signs and warnings of our bodies and emotions.

If ignored or mismanaged, these prolonged periods of unnurtured fatigue and pain can lead to the closing down of our emotional responses, which is the condition known as "burnout." It is a survival reaction. Often when people say they are suffering from burnout, they are really experiencing extreme symptoms of pain and fatigue that can be healed if faced in time. As long as we are hurting badly and caring deeply, we are not yet burned out. Part of the spiritual life is to become sensitive to the signals our bodies and feelings give us that healing is needed. The deeper Christians grow in compassion toward others, the more important it is that they face their inner selves with compassion. It seems to be a spiritual law that sooner or later we treat others as we treat our own inner selves.

There is something that can be done. Slowly but also deeply, many churches are becoming aware of the vast, as yet almost unexplored, powers of prayer that can touch us, heal us, transform us at levels of which we have hardly dared to dream. This is one of the supreme signs of the Holy Spirit.

Yes, and these powers of prayer also transform the world through us. Prayer does not merely lead us to action; prayer itself is action. Jesus spoke of the kingdom of God coming with power like yeast, like wind, and like light (Matt. 5:14; 13:33; John 3:8). When we unite with God's love through deep and honest prayer, we become direct and open channels of that healing love to a world in pain. Every time we pray in depth, the world around us, as well as the world within us, undergoes change.

This book is a witness to my belief that the passion and compassion of God's spirit reveals that each of us is uniquely and limitlessly loved (loved as if each were the only child in creation) and that all inner wounds, no matter how deep or pervasive, can be touched and transformed. It is also my belief that God's passionate compassion will reveal to us, as we are being made whole, ever-deeper levels of the hurt and hunger in the world around us.

I do not believe that once our eyes are opened, we will fall back into a complacent sleep. Nor do I believe that our inner wounds, once healed, will be forgotten and wasted. God's spirit wastes nothing! We are told in the twentieth chapter of John that the risen Jesus showed Thomas and the other disciples his wounds. I used to wonder why those wounds remained on his risen body of light. Why weren't those earthly marks of suffering swallowed up, forgotten, in glory? Was it so his friends could identify him? Partly. But I think there was a more important reason. I think all his friends through the ages to come were being shown that wounds, especially when healed, can become sources and signs of new radiance of life. No longer the sources of pain and despair, the wounds now healed can become the channels of healing for others.

Think of some inner wound in your own life that is now healed. Would you for any reason give up the new power to love and to understand that you have learned?

God does not send us pain. God is not a wounder or punisher. This is important to understand as our trust in God grows. But neither does God let our wound be wasted. The Comforter, the Holy Spirit, will not remove the lines of hard-won experience from our faces. A new power of light, the light of the divine passionate compassion, will shine through those lines on our faces.

CHAPTER TWO

The Prayer That Nurtures

God, the eternal healer, the eternal lover, offers to touch our tiredness, our stress, and our pain. The most direct response to this love, the widest door we can open, is through the relationship we call prayer. For it is a relationship and not primarily a discipline.

Most of our problems with prayer arise from our tendency to turn spiritual growing into a set of laws or a gymnastic exercise. I have seen great inner struggle, fatigue, and guilt result when we treat prayer like a discipline.

I recently talked with a young woman who had been trying diligently to turn her spiritual life into a set of rules. She had structured her whole prayer life. She had rules about what time of day she prayed, where she prayed, what position she would take when she prayed, how long she prayed. She felt she always had to begin with adoration, then move on to confession, and follow with petition, intercession, thanksgiving, and commitment—in that fixed order. She tried to exclude all distractions, because she considered the prayer invalid if her mind wandered, and she closely monitored every sign of progress. She was exhausted!

Being human, she would often fail to live up to her own rules, and then she would feel guilty. Or if she did live up to her rules, she got so tired and bored that she would skip prayer for several days and feel even guiltier. She constantly felt she was letting God down and betraying her deeper self.

As we talked together, extraordinary relief came into her face as she slowly realized that she was being much harder on herself than God was. She realized that God is asking for relatedness, not rules.

"After all," she told me, laughing, "I don't feel that I have to sit down with my husband in the same place at the same time every day and bring up the same subjects in the same order! Sometimes we just sit in loving silence together. Sometimes we have a deep, long sharing. Sometimes we exchange a quick hug and a smile."

"And sometimes," I responded, "you want to share some interesting activity together, and feel the loving presence of the other. Sometimes you might want to take a walk with your loved one and see the world anew through the eyes of your companion.

"If you felt you had to move through a strict structure and order in each conversation before you got around to what was really on your mind, I suspect that your conversations would dry up and cease in a very short time."

If this is true of our relationships, it is certainly true of prayer. When we pray, we are relating to Somebody—the supreme Somebody. But as with any healthy relationship, it can't be turned into a set of laws, even good laws. Any relationship that remains whole is based on a commitment of ongoing trust, which expresses itself in varying and growing ways all our lives.

It is best to have some form of deliberate opening to God each day, but we need not be troubled if the form and expression change. That is as it should be. God's love is a growing personal relatedness in which we are loved and challenged to love without limit. *This transforming friendship always nurtures before it challenges as well as during the challenge.*

In the previous chapter, we looked at Jesus kneeling before his disciples, offering them an act of personal service. Look now at the risen Jesus in John 21. Before he challenged Peter to feed the hungry sheep of the world, he filled the disciples' nets full and cooked and served them breakfast on the beach. He fed those hungry, tired "shepherds" first.

Just as he knew they could not wash the feet of others, with all that implies, until they themselves had been ministered to, so they could not be sent as nurturing shepherds to the hungering, hurting world until they had been comforted, fed, given strength and the assurance of his presence, the Bread of Life always with them.

This is hard for us. It is hard to learn to receive. We like to be on the giving end. We like to be in control. It is not easy to admit that we are vulnerable, that we have needs, limits, and wounds. It is hard to admit it to others, and it is hard to admit it to God. Perhaps it is hardest of all to admit it to ourselves.

In a prayer group to which I once belonged, it was the custom to raise our hands during the intercession period if we felt the need for special prayers from the group and for the laying on of hands. It was literally years before I could bring myself to indicate to the group that sometimes I needed special prayers, special help. And yet, I often prayed for others and joined in the healing ministry for them. Was it pride? Was it the fear of being selfish? Was it the wish not to be conspicuous? Was it the feeling that no one, including God, ought to be bothered with my little problems? Was it a wish to be on the controlling end, to be the giver rather than the receiver? It was probably a combination of all these feelings. But whatever the reasons, until I could admit to myself, to God, to my loving group that I too sometimes felt weak and in need, the deep relationships could not grow.

How can we most directly experience the transforming nurture of God through prayer? There is a form of prayer I love to share especially with persons who are in deep stress, fatigued, drained of energy, ill, or convalescent. Indeed, I recommend it for everyone, no matter how healthy, if only for a few minutes every day. It is a prayer of deep healing, regenerating power. It is a prayer closely involved with the body as well as the emotions and the whole spirit. It can be a prayer of only a few minutes or a prayer of a whole hour or more. It is the most radical form of healing prayer I know.

There are two parts to this prayer, one I have known

about for many years and the other has just recently come to me as a strong, guiding gift from God. You may feel more drawn to one aspect than to the other. Or you may wish to combine them. Trust your feelings and your inner readiness; never push yourself into any form of prayer that does not seem right for you.

The first part of this prayer is often called "soaking prayer." I personally use the image of light, but some people prefer the images of water, wind, color, healing hands, wings, and so on. In this prayer, we do not ask for anything special. We just rest, let go, breathe in, and soak up the healing light of God which embraces us. We may not feel anything special; nevertheless it is a profoundly physical form of prayer in which every cell and organ of our bodies is washed, filled, and renewed in the healing light of God's love. Some people do feel warmth, waves of energy, a tingling sensation. Others have no such physical reactions. But the action of the light is a reality whether or not we immediately register it. We do not feel the ultraviolet rays of the sun, but they pervade us and affect our bodies whenever we go out into the daylight. Similarly, when we deliberately open ourselves to the healing presence of God, the deep action of divine love flows into every part of our lives. In this prayer we rest in it, breathe it, and allow it to work its transforming renewal within us. If thoughts wander, don't worry. Let them play like children in the sun.

The second part of this prayer, the prayer that is a new joy in my life, might be called the "prayer of the heart." It is a deeply incarnational form of prayer based on Jesus' parable of the yeast expanding within the bread (Matt. 13:33). Just as the soaking prayer envisages the light surrounding us and flowing through us, so this prayer envisages the healing power expanding from within. The heart is the symbol of the central energy flow of our bodies, just as it is the symbol, through the ages, of the deep center of God's love. In this prayer we are joining our physical and emotional need for renewal with the deep incarnational union between our hearts and God's heart.

Soaking Prayer

How precious is thy steadfast love, O God!
  The children of men take refuge in the shadow of thy
    wings.
They feast on the abundance of thy house,
  and thou givest them drink from the river of thy
    delights.
For with thee is the fountain of life;
  in thy light do we see light.

—Psalm 36:7–9

Sit or lie in a relaxed position, and give thanks to God
that "underneath are the everlasting arms" (Deut. 33:27).
Put this time of prayer under Christ's spirit. Breathe gently
and slowly, letting your hands remain open in a relaxed way.
Image a cloud of light forming around your body. (Don't
expect to see this light with physical eyes. Very few people
do. But by your inward imaging, you are claiming the healing light of God that is always offered to you.) Perhaps you
may image the light strong and intense or perhaps gently
luminous. Perhaps it may seem to have a restful or energiz-
ing color.

Rest, and gently breathe in this surrounding light. Picture it flowing through the top of your head, slowly flowing
through your tight facial muscles, relaxing them, especially
around your eyes and jaw. Picture it now as a river of light
quietly flowing through your whole body, calming, relaxing, releasing every part. Think of every slow, light breath
as if breathing the breath of life which God breathes into
every living being. If you wish, repeat from the psalm
quoted above: "For with thee is the fountain of life;/in thy
light do we see light."

If the light image is not right for you, think of God's
healing water flowing around your body or of a gentle wind
blowing through you. These are also biblical symbols.

Prayer of the Heart

Place both hands, palms down, over your heart. (Your
heart is central in your chest, under the breastbone.) Keep

your hands on your heart in a relaxed position for a minute or two, and then say aloud or inwardly in silence, very slowly, with long pauses between each phrase: "The living heart of Jesus Christ is taking form within my heart . . . filling . . . calming . . . restoring . . . bringing new life." (Take a quiet pause, while you envision a warm light glowing in your heart.) "And this new life in my blood flows peacefully, with full healing power through my whole body." At this point you may feel like gently laying your hands on any part of your body that seems to need special help, and you may envision the new current of life through the transformed circulation flowing into that area.

When it seems right, open your hands, palms outward, and say: "And the power of this new life flows into my actions and relationships with others this day."

Then return your hands to your heart, giving thanks in the name of Christ, perhaps praying the beautiful words: "My heart and flesh sing for joy to the living God" (Psalm 84:2).

It is important that this prayer is not hurried. Move through it as slowly as feels natural. As you grow with it, you will probably wish to let it form its own timing.

I have found in myself a spontaneous wish to pray the first part, the soaking prayer, at night just before sleeping, and the second part, the prayer of the heart, in the morning just before getting up and again just before some stressful task or encounter. You may prefer a different rhythm, or some other form of nurturing, restoring prayer may be suggested to you. For example, some people wish to speak aloud or inwardly a special word or phrase that seems to bring to them vividly the love of God. Others may wish to relax and gaze at some special picture or object that symbolizes God's nearness. Some may wish to relax in a chair, close their eyes, and say, "Loving God, I need you," and let the symbolic images or words form spontaneously.

Whatever form seems right to you in your prayer of

receiving, remember three things. First, you do not need to beg or plead with God. Prayer is a response to the love already forever given to us. God is far more ready to hear and to give than we are to speak or to receive. God loves us even when we cannot feel love for God. God hears us even when we cannot speak. God meets us even when we are not worthy to be met. God holds us in the healing hands even when we lie down helplessly on them. Our willpower, our articulate prayers, and our structuring do not heal us. Healing comes from our growing responsive trust in the limitless love that always embraces us, whether or not we feel and wish for it.

Second, remember that because this is a living relationship with God and not a set of rules, your forms and methods of communication with God will change, evolve, expand, flow in new ways. Don't make a prison out of any method or let anyone else (even if that person is someone you admire and consider to be spiritually advanced) impose on you any method or symbolism that does not seem right, natural, or helpful to you. Listen instead to the gentle guidance of the Holy Spirit within who searches the deep places in your heart and prays for you and through you.

Third, be gentle toward yourself. Sometimes you will have wandering thoughts, distractions during prayer. Don't fight them or force them down. Perhaps they are signals of deep wounded areas within that will need attention as you move into the prayers of memory healing. If they surface during nurturing prayer, envision yourself lifting them lovingly and putting them into the healing hands of Jesus Christ. If they seem trivial distractions, don't use force. Smile at them as you would at a little child or animal at play, and return to the Center while they play at the edges of your consciousness.

You won't always feel deep love for God or deep longing for prayer. There are seasons of the spirit just as there are seasons during the year. As with any committed friendship, there will be times when you feel much emotional concentration on the other and times when you feel blank and dry. This does not weaken or invalidate the prayer in the least. Some of the most powerful times of prayer are the times when with humor and honesty we admit to God that at the moment we feel dry, bored, not in the mood, and yet, nevertheless, we are willing to be reached and nurtured. Great miracles of opening and change within can happen in these times.

If every day, no matter what your mood, you allow the love of God to feed you deeply through some form of soaking prayer, if only for a few minutes, I believe amazing changes will happen in your life. God, whose name is love, offers us—with every breath we take—a new, transforming energy for our tense, stress-filled bodies and an inner healing that reaches depths we had not dreamed!

CHAPTER THREE

With Christ to the Painful Past

Think of an experience, recent or long past, serious or trivial, that still causes you pain, anger, shock, or sorrow. Perhaps it was someone's death. Perhaps a friend misunderstood and turned against you. Perhaps you were told that your job contract would not be renewed or that some work in which you had done your best was not acceptable. Perhaps the doctor told you bad news about your health. Perhaps you were asked for a divorce. Perhaps your house was robbed. Maybe you recall some physical shock—a car accident, a sudden illness, a house fire, a disastrous storm, a painful fall, a personal assault. Or you might be thinking of some apparently trivial grief, humiliation, or failure in childhood or the teenaged years. You wonder why it hurts after all this time.

We all can think of such wounds from the past. Some are genuinely healed, but others, for some reason, still burn and fester deep within our memories. We have tried to understand, to forgive, to release. But years later we realize (when we take an honest look at the deep places) that the trauma is as fresh and hurtful as if it had happened yesterday. We wonder why we can't release it, and we wonder what damage the inner, festering hurt is doing to our bodies, our lives, our relationships.

It seems worse when the repeating tape within is not a sudden shock, but a memory of long, drawn out pain extending through many years. Perhaps you felt unwanted, unnurtured in childhood, or you can recall an unusually difficult adjustment in adolescence. Was it a wounding, destructive marriage? Are you thinking of a distressing job experience? Have you felt a victim of racial injustice? Have you experienced years of alienation from family members?

The little boy or girl, the adolescent, the young man or woman, the person you were just yesterday still lives within you. This inner self may still be in shock or fear or may still be weeping in lonely grief. If this inner self of the past is nurtured, comforted, and healed, it becomes a released and integrated part of your total self, contributing to the rich fullness of your whole personality. But if at some point in your life the person you were has been emotionally unnurtured, traumatized, or wounded, and healing has not taken place, then your integrated growth is not complete. At that point, your development has been arrested. Other aspects of the self may grow, but in that area there is a vortex of pain, hunger, anger, self-doubt, and shock that will eventually affect the whole person.

Whenever I am asked to lead a church retreat or workshop, I try to make time for the participants to face and share some of their inner pain (if they wish to do so). I am always amazed at the load of unhealed pain that so many good church members, deeply religious and sincere men and women, carry around with them. Not only are they carrying a burden of pain, but usually they feel guilty that they are still hurting. Does this mean, they wonder, that they have not truly forgiven? Does it mean that they are not trusting God?

Once an older man came to talk with me about the pain he had experienced for several years when he discovered his wife had been unfaithful to him. He was a long-standing church member and a sincere believer in prayer and the love of God. He couldn't understand why he couldn't really forgive his wife and let the past go.

"I love her," he told me, with tears in his eyes. "I never wanted a divorce. She's a wonderful woman in so many ways, and I know I was partly to blame. But I can't let it go. I can't stop thinking about it. I'm still resentful, even though I want to forgive. I've prayed and prayed about it, and it doesn't seem to make any difference. But we're told by Jesus that we must forgive. Well, I've tried, but it just doesn't happen."

As we shared and talked together, it became clear to us both after a while that by his wish to forgive, his willingness, he had in fact forgiven her. But the *feeling* of forgiveness and release would probably not come until his pain had been healed.

This realization was wonderfully new to me. Since that time I have talked with many people who feel guiltily that they have not forgiven someone who hurt them, when actually what they are feeling is unhealed pain. When the deep inner healing has begun, usually the old feelings of persisting anger and resentment melt swiftly away.

We are so apt to forget that most of Jesus' ministry was healing, healing of all kinds. It still is!

No wound is so trivial that the love of God is not concerned with it. No pain is so deep, so long-standing, that the love of God cannot reach it. Every shock, every bleeding wound, every anger and grief is not only encompassed by that love but is also held and transformed by that love. The fact that it is in what we call the "past" makes no difference to the power of God's love. All times are open and present to that unsleeping, all-embracing Consciousness. God asks only our willingness.

Suggested Prayer: *Prayer for Early Memories*

Jesus said, "Let the children come to me, and do not hinder them; for to such belongs the kingdom of heaven."
                                                    —Matthew 19:14

Beloved, let us love one another; for love is of God. . . .
There is no fear in love, but perfect love casts out fear. . . .
We love, because he first loved us.
                                                    —1 John 4:7, 18–19

Visualize the risen Jesus Christ coming to you. Let him

come to you in whatever form and way is best for you. He may seem to be in the form of a loved and trusted friend. Or he may seem to come in one of the usual ways our churches picture him. Or he may seem to come as light filling the room. If you have called on his name as the embodied spirit of divine love, you can trust what inner image or symbol comes. If no special inner image seems to come, just relax, knowing Jesus Christ is with you anyway. Sit quietly, allowing a feeling of comfort and peace to enclose you.

Now quietly turn to a hurtful memory, whether new or old. Visualizing Jesus with you, walk back to that place in time, back to that house, that room. Now visualize the part in you that was hurt as if it were a little child coming forth from you. Picture this little wounded child within you going to Jesus in that room, that place, and being comforted by him in some way that seems right for you.

Now picture the person (or persons) also closely involved in that wounding experience coming to that room or that place. Jesus turns with you to meet him or her. Now the inner hurt of the other person comes forth as if it were a wounded child, too. (Even if a parent, a teacher, a spouse, or an employer is part of your wound, visualize the little child in that individual.) This child in the other is touched, held, comforted in some way by the Christ. Hold this picture for a few moments, and give thanks. See if you can visualize your inner child and the other inner child embracing or becoming reconciled in some way. (If you cannot do that yet, do not force it. You can come back another time.) When it seems right, visualize leaving your own inner child and that of the other together there in the presence of Jesus. Return to the room where you are sitting, knowing that Christ's presence is with you here as well.

Give thanks, and conclude the prayer.

There are many alternative forms of the prayer for the healing of a memory. You may find the inner imagery spontaneously changing, even when returning to the same memory. If you need to go back to one memory several times, you will probably uncover new and deeper levels of shock, pain, and fear that you had not fully faced or experienced before. God, in mercy, usually does not allow us to see the real pain and depth of what we experienced until the healing is already well under way. You will not be allowed to experience more of this pain than you, together with Christ, can handle.

Sometimes you will find that you simply don't want to walk back to a memory, even with the presence of Christ. Trust that feeling, and do not force anything. I was helped on this point by a student who told me that when she felt that inner shrinking and reluctance, she would visualize Jesus walking alone into that room or that place, putting the whole memory under his light to soak. She would not try to follow him or visualize the details of that memory at that time but would let it soak for several days or weeks. Sometimes that would be all that was needed for healing. Sometimes she would feel led, later on, to return to that experience. She found she could do it without reluctance then.

I find it helpful each night to think of some experience of difficulty that happened during the day and to visualize Jesus putting healing hands on that moment, transforming it. In this way, hurts and wounds do not accumulate.

As for memories longer past, I don't feel that I have to move through a special memory each day. But I try not to let a week go by without a deliberate turning to a healing experience of a wound. Sometimes a memory will rise spontaneously. Sometimes I have to search a bit. Sometimes I ask God to summon forth a memory whose time for healing has come, and often I am surprised at what surfaces.

As with the nurturing prayers discussed earlier, it is important to remember that we are not creating God's healing love for our inner self because we are now praying about it. This love has always been around us, embracing us. Rather, by such prayers we are claiming it, internalizing it, allowing its transforming power to intensify in our lives.

As one by one the inner children of your hurting memories are comforted and healed, they are gently brought into creative union with the rest of the person you are. You become more whole as these pockets of pain are cleansed and filled with new light and health. You do not, perhaps, forget your former experiences, but in the divine ecology of God they become (as with Jesus' wounds) no longer sources of fragmentation. They become sources of compassionate light and healing for others.

CHAPTER FOUR

With Christ to Deep, Forgotten Pain

What if we don't know what is hurting us? What if we can't identify the source of our pain? What if the trauma happened before we could think coherently, or it was so painful that we pushed it into the subconscious self where we would not have to look at it? What if the fear and pain are associated with some deep, ongoing conflict we cannot name or identify? Does that mean we can't experience healing of these hurts because we can't remember or identify them?

As I explained in the introduction, this book was not meant to supplant any necessary or helpful psychological therapy through which God's healing love also works. But in my specialized ministry of depth prayer workshops and personal counseling I have both experienced and observed profound transformations taking place when we allow God's healing power to take possession of the forgotten areas of pain and fear through the prayers of healing imagery.

Sometimes it is a direct fear based on an early forgotten incident. For example, for years I froze inwardly if a dog ran toward me, even if it was friendly. I couldn't understand why I felt this way because I couldn't remember any bad experiences with dogs. But it was a real, extremely uncomfortable feeling, and it was certainly spoiling my pleasure in taking walks. Then one day my mother laughingly told me how a tiny terrier knocked me over in the snow when I was a toddler and how surprised we both looked as we went over in the drifts. I hadn't shown any special shock at the time, and she hadn't realized how profoundly it had affected me over many years.

That personal example is simple compared with other, more serious, and long-lasting traumas. It is probable that most of our fears, unexplained angers, aversions, and attractions have their roots in early experiences of deprivation, loneliness, pain, or lack of nurture.

Our feelings about ourselves and other people, our feelings about the friendliness or hostility of the world surrounding us, our very feelings about God stem from experiences that came our way before we could talk or think logically.

Take, for example, the experiences of babies two generations ago who were not held, cuddled, or fed off schedule by their mothers because many doctors at that time felt such spontaneous handling was bad for them. One elderly woman told me she distinctly remembers standing by the crib of her crying infant son, holding a watch in her hand, crying as hard as he was because it wasn't yet three o'clock in the afternoon and she had been told to pick him up only every three hours! Perhaps that baby was emotionally tough enough not to be harmed. But if he was a sensitive person, the rigid schedule during his first year of life, the lack of nurturing handling, might have given him a deep, despairing feeling that life would never provide what he needed and that nothing would ever answer his call. If his family was a loving one, as he grew older he would find no rational reason for his inner anxiousness and sadness. For years he would wonder why he felt that way about other people.

Even the birth experience itself has probably been traumatic for most of us. Individuals who have had a near-death experience say, almost without exception, that it is an easy, gentle thing to die. Not so with birth! Those who have undergone hypnotism and recalled birth experiences usually report strain, fear, anger, and shock as they emerge from the struggle of labor. They have passed in a short time from darkness to glaring light, from silence or muted noise to what must seem like a hideous din, from a warm enclosure to cold, frightening space. Instantly they must learn to manage breathing air. All this is part of a normal birth. If there were complications with the labor or delivery, if instruments had to be used, if there was difficulty in getting the breathing started, all contribute extra shock and strain to the system. Probably we never go through anything half so difficult again! (I am interested in some of the experiments in what is called "gentle childbirth" in which light and noise are held to a minimum and the child is immediately held and warmed. Observers of this method say the babies have a peaceful expression, and after the first cry as they draw the first breath, they usually do not cry much more.) Who knows what burdens we may be carrying on our spirits because of early, unhealed shock as we came into the world?

Perhaps we experience some other kind of suppression. We may recall some early, difficult incident of our childhood, but we can't recall any special feeling about it. We may distinctly remember the death of a beloved pet, for example, or the death of a close family member, but we can't remember any emotional response. We may remember being punished unjustly at home or at school, but we can't recall any special pain or anger. Most likely we *did* have strong feelings but did not allow them to surface into our conscious memory. Nevertheless, they existed below the surface and probably affected many of our attitudes and feelings about other things. There are crying children deep within us!

God's love and God's power to heal are not limited by the limits of our memory. God's transforming healing can reach into the deepest roots, into the most buried, forgotten areas of pain.

We are told in Psalm 139: "If I make my bed in Sheol, thou art there!" *Sheol* is the Hebrew word, like the Greek word *Hades*, that means "the place of shadows, dimness, half-aliveness, the area of the forgotten or dimly remembered." It is an excellent word for our own subconscious selves, where life-forming experiences are forgotten or only dimly, perhaps symbolically, remembered.

But God's love is already there. The healing through

the incarnated Christ, the embodied love of God, can enter that shadowy pain with full power.

There are two forms of prayer by which I have experienced the deep opening of buried pain to the healing of God. One of these images the loving Christ moving directly to the deep self with his light and healing hands. The other takes us deliberately through the various stages of early life, babyhood through childhood, opening areas we suspect are the bases of our problems to the healing action of Christ. These prayers can be experienced either with a group or alone, but perhaps in some cases it is wiser first to pray for the subconscious self in the context of a loving, supportive group in which all members are also opening their depth selves.

Suggested Prayer One: *Prayer for the Subconscious*

> If I say, "Let only darkness cover me,
>   and the light about me be night,"
> even the darkness is not dark to thee,
>   the night is bright as the day;
>   for darkness is as light with thee.
> —Psalm 139:11–12

Picture the Christ coming to you in whatever way seems best for you. The nurturing light fills the room, and you feel safe and comforted in that presence. Together, you and Jesus walk to the door that opens to your deep self. (It can be a door in the floor or in the wall, or you can image instead going into a cave or some other symbol for your subconscious self.) With your consent, Jesus opens the door and goes into the unknown depth that is you, carrying his full light and radiant love. *Do not try to follow him or to see what he sees in your depth.* You, your conscious self, remain outside the door, giving thanks. Affirm in faith that Jesus Christ now moves throughout your deepest levels of emotional experience and finds the children of your pain who were so deeply submerged that you could no longer hear them crying. The living Christ is laying healing hands on them, embracing them, comforting them.

Nothing will be destroyed, but bit by bit all will be transformed. Perhaps you will feel asked to look at some particular thing. Perhaps some special memory will float to the surface. But most of the time you will feel nothing special at first.

Thankfully affirm that the living Christ is also releasing the newborn "children" within, new gifts and powers ready now to be born from your depths.

After a while, you may feel that Jesus comes up the stairs again. Or perhaps you may feel that you are to hold the image of his staying below for a while. Trust your feeling. When it seems right to conclude your prayer, ask that the entrance to your subconscious, the depth self, be especially sealed and protected by Christ's own light, so that from now on only the Holy Spirit or those who come in his name may enter that deepest self.

Remember again, the use of such imagery in prayer is not changing God's mind or summoning God to do errands. By this inner consent and by this symbolic realism we are cooperating with God and enabling God to intensify the work of healing love.

Suggested Prayer Two: *Prayer for the Early Life*

For thou didst form my inward parts,
thou didst knit me together in my mother's womb.
. . . .
Thou knowest me right well;
my frame was not hidden from thee,
when I was being made in secret.
—Psalm 139:13–15

Thou art he who took me from the womb;
 thou didst keep me safe upon my mother's breasts.
Upon thee was I cast from my birth,
 and since my mother bore me thou hast been my God.
                                    —Psalm 22:9–10

Unborn Infancy: Visualize the healing love of God, the light of God, enfolding the small embryo that was you. Let the warm, nurturing hands of love nurture you deeply. You are held and carried by God.

Birth Experience: If you have reason to suspect that your birth experience was difficult and traumatic, picture your newborn, little body in the act of birth, being received now by God's own hands. Picture that small body being gently drawn into life, the breath of life being breathed into your mouth, your small body being held in warmth, strength, infinite delight, and welcome.

Early Days of Life: If you have reason to believe that your first vulnerable days were hurtful, if you were given up for adoption, if you were separated from closeness to your parents, if you had a physical problem, if your parents, because of their own inner wounds, were not able to show warm love, if you were a disappointment to them or a burden to them, then picture the small baby that was you lifted and held within the arms of Christ. You are being held as long as you need it. You are being delighted in. You can be made to feel that you have a special place forever within the heart of God, who is both the Father and the Mother, forever strong, forever nurturing.

Childhood: Now conscious memories begin. If you suspect there were many times of fear, humiliation, timidity, and inferiority that you have buried, picture yourself as the little boy or girl you were. Feel the closeness and reassurance of Christ's companionship. Let yourself be told that you are accepted, safe, and special. Accept the challenging love of

Christ which offers to you as the little child release for your own special gift, beauty, and powers. Visualize the child being released in full emotional response and spontaneity.

Conclude the prayer with thanksgiving that God through Christ rejoices in reliving for you those poignant times of transition, so that which has been a source of fear and fragmentation begins to heal and may become centers of beauty, release, and compassion.

In such praying are we merely descending into self-pity? Is this merely self-preoccupied introspection, when we ought to be forgetting our selves with the healing of the world? On the contrary, as God heals us at our depths, we will perhaps for the first time be released from the prison of self-pity. More than we realize, our inner energies far below the surface have been dominated and drained by the power of our forgotten pain. As our inner healing grows, glows, expands, we will be astonished at the new energies released within us. We will be increasingly set free to come near to others and to be sensitive to the needs and hurts of others. By allowing God to love us back to health, we will be enabled to love others to an extent we had never dared before.

After several weeks (or maybe even days) of regular prayer for the deep self, you will probably notice other changes. Your dreams may change. You may notice a change in physical health. Perhaps some stubborn bodily symptoms will give way for the first time. You may notice that some deeply ingrained habits, such as compulsive eating, drinking, smoking, buying, or talking, begin to change. Maybe some phobias lose their force. You look at things in a different way. Other people don't seem so unfriendly or annoying.

Some memories will surface. They can be dealt with as with any prayer for a conscious memory. Most of them will not surface, and it is a mistake to try to force yourself to remember them. Leave in God's hands the early emotions you will recall. In any case, the prayer for the deep, forgotten self is one of the most radically transforming actions offered to us. Its action within is truly as the yeast within the loaf of which Jesus spoke (Matt. 13:33).

This is a prayer of the profoundest faith, even though we feel nothing at first, for it is increasing dependence upon the will of God who longs to heal us far more than we long to be healed. God does not knock down the doors of our resistance; God waits for the beginning of our response and for the radical action of our consent. If our consent, our willingness, is minuscule, anxious, or reluctant, great miracles can happen even through the tiniest offering!

CHAPTER FIVE

With Christ to the Uncertain Future

Another kind of wound is the fear of the future. Many people I meet at retreats tell me that it is a struggle, even after the healing of past memories, not to feel anxious about what lies ahead.

"My painful memories about my childhood are being touched and healed," one woman told me. "But next week my sister will be coming for a visit, and I'm already worrying about it. I'm afraid we'll get upset and angry with each other again, and then we'll repeat the old patterns and make *new* wounds."

We can all think of similar anxieties.

"I'm going to the doctor tomorrow, and I'm worried about what she'll tell me."

"This job interview is coming up, and I really feel tense about it."

"When I make that speech tomorrow, I know I'll shake all over. I always do!"

Maybe it's not a specific fear but a rather diffuse, general worry. It is none the less painful for that.

"I worry about being a parent. How do I know I'll be adequate for my children?"

"I'm always worrying about my health and thinking I'm going to be seriously ill."

"The thought of old age and its helplessness really scares me."

"How do I know I'll be wise and courageous when trouble really hits? I might go all to pieces!"

"Nobody will ever want to marry me. I know when I meet someone I really like I'll probably mess it up."

Probably most of these anxieties have their roots in the unhealed past. Frequently the prayer for the healing of the subconscious self affects profoundly our feelings about the future. But that is not always the case. When we have been hurt once, it is natural to fear the hurt again. And if we do not fear any special thing in itself, we are often afraid of *being* afraid.

It comes as a surprising joy to many people to realize that the power of God's healing love encompasses not only the past but also the future. God's love can transform not only the wound of the past into a source of new strength but also the potential wound of the future. Again, we are told in Psalm 139: "Thou dost beset me *behind* and *before,*/and layest thy hand upon me" (italics added). What we call the "future" is no barrier to God's love.

I began to get an inkling of this in the 1950s when I heard the great Methodist preacher, Leslie Weatherhead, declare: "God will meet you at every corner you come to." But the full implications of what he said took twenty-five years to develop in my thinking, living, and praying.

I first tried this form of prayer when I began to worry about a large class I was scheduled to teach. Though I had taught many classes through the years, for some reason I was worried about this one. I felt inadequate and somewhat intimidated. On the day of the first class, I was sitting in my office, trying to relax in soaking prayer, visualizing the light of God's love surrounding me. Then the thought came to me: *How would it be if I visualized this healing light filling the classroom itself, right now, before the class meets? How would it be if I asked Christ to go ahead of me into that room, touching and welcoming all who enter it, including me?*

I made this prayer as clear and specific as I could, just as with the healing of a specific memory. I asked the risen Jesus to walk into that room where soon I would be and to fill it with his light and warm strength, to bless and heal the experience to come. Of course I knew that God's love was already in that room, even before I prayed about it. God's love is always everywhere. But by this form of symbolic, imaging prayer, I was able to enter more fully and intensely into that experience of love and claim it as a reality in my life.

The relaxed, *healed* strength seemed to wash over me like a warm wave when I entered the classroom a half hour later. I felt comforted, enabled. As the students came in, there was a feeling of warm friendliness among us. I felt as if we all, teacher and students alike, were held in the same light, the same embrace.

Naturally, as in every challenging situation, there were problems to be faced and worked through. There was a lot of hard work to be done. The presence of Christ does not release us from problem solving and hard work. The Lord is there not to remove real challenges but to enable us to meet them with serene power. But all feeling of panicky inadequacy was gone. When I found myself beginning to worry lest the feeling would return, I would visualize anew the risen Christ entering that room, taking charge of us all within it, blessing and fulfilling the events to come.

But what about the more general fears we can't seem to pin down to anything specific? What about the fears of loneliness, health problems, old age, facing death someday, general uncertainty about jobs and relationships? With these fears, we can't visualize any special room, any special time. So how can we release this sort of anxiety into the hands of Christ?

I often think of Jesus' promise to his disciples at the Last Supper on the night before his death:

In my Father's house are many rooms; if it were not so, would I have told you that I go to prepare a place for you? And when I go and prepare a place for you, I will come again and will take you to myself, that where I am you may be also.
—John 14:2–3

I believe he was talking not only to his disciples about his death and what lies after but also to all of us, his friends in all ages to come. He was promising that any place to which we were called and led, he would not only go *with* us but also go *before* us, preparing the way and the place. Wherever we were, we would be in his presence.

These "rooms" (or "mansions," as the older translations put it) are the infinite dimensions and expressions of God's love. They involve this world, this space and time as well as worlds and dimensions we cannot yet see.

With these vague, diffuse fears of the far future to come, though we cannot specifically visualize a place or time, we can pray a prayer very similar to that of the prayer for the subconscious. We image the Lord walking ahead of us into unknown territory and turning with a smile to let us know that all is well and under healing control. With the growing experience of this prayer, we will increasingly feel that the unknown future is in his hands, and we will increasingly feel the blessing of the unknown future flowing warmly and with healing toward us *now*, here in the present.

Suggested Prayer One: *Prayer for the Future*

Thou dost beset me behind and before,
   and layest thy hand upon me.
Whither shall I go from thy Spirit?
   Or whither shall I flee from thy presence?
If I ascend to heaven, thou art there!
   If I make my bed in Sheol, thou art there!
If I take the wings of the morning
   and dwell in the uttermost parts of the sea,
even there thy hand shall lead me,
   and thy right hand shall hold me.
                              —Psalm 139:5, 7–10

Relax, close your eyes, and visualize Jesus Christ coming into the room, in whatever form is best for you. Relax and breathe in his presence and light. Now together look at some specific point in the time ahead, at an experience to come.

Visualize the Lord, in confidence and strength, walking ahead of you and entering that business office, that classroom, that doctor's office, that pulpit, that home, that airplane, that committee room. Watch him moving around that room, that place, touching it, lifting his hands in healing and blessing, filling every corner with his light.

Now visualize him turning to look at you with a smile, giving you the awareness that when you enter that place, you (and those with you) will feel his presence, his comfort, and his guidance. He will be there to welcome you when you get there.

Give thanks, turn your attention again to the place where you are now, knowing that the future event is in good hands. Conclude your prayer.

Suggested Prayer Two: *Prayer for the Future*

Jesus said, "In my Father's house are many rooms; if it were not so, would I have told you that I go to prepare a place for you?"

—John 14:2

Relax, close your eyes. Visualize the Lord entering the room. You sit together quietly for a while, and then he invites you to walk with him through the rooms of a spacious, beautiful house.

The house has many rooms, full of light and fresh air. Finally you come to a room whose door is still closed. Perhaps it has a name on it, such as my future health, my future work, my future relationships, or my old age. He asks if you are willing for him to open the door and go into the room to bless it.

If you consent, he opens the door, and leaving it open, he enters the room and fills it with a radiant light. You remain standing on the threshold and do not try to enter. All you can see is that healing, beautiful light, and you hear his voice, "I have prepared this place for you. When someday you enter this door, you will feel warmly welcomed, ready, and expectant."

Now visualize the Lord coming out of the room. The door remains open, and the light flows out of the room, already surrounding you with warmth. Together, you and the Lord walk back to your present place. The warm light still surrounds you in the present.

Conclude your prayer with thanksgiving. You might think again of the words of Jesus: "When I go and prepare a place for you, I will come again and take you to myself, that where I am you may be also" (John 14:3).

You will soon discover how often you wish to pray this prayer. The prayer for the specific event ahead might well be a prayer for each night and each morning as you think of tasks to come. The prayer for the more distant, uncertain future may not need to be prayed so often. Let God's spirit guide you in whatever rhythm of prayer is best for you.

CHAPTER SIX

Depth Prayer for Our Central Inner Problem

We each have a special problem child within. It underlies our surface perplexities, deeper than our unhealed memories (though usually interwoven with our memories) affecting our relationships, and blocks our relationship with God and the fuller life. We each know there is a central place, a central pain, from which arises most of our problems.

"I'm frightened most of the time," a woman in middle life once told me. "I think I was *born* scared! Oh, I don't think most people notice it. A lot of the time I forget about it myself. It doesn't outwardly interfere with my everyday life. But when I'm being honest with myself, I know most of my decisions are based on the questions: 'Will I be hurt?' 'Is it dangerous?' 'What will happen to me?' It's as if there was a scared little girl deep down in there who feels timid and shy and worried all the time, who has never grown up!"

An older man once shared with me his problem with anger. "As far back as I can remember, I have felt belligerent deep down inside. One of my earliest memories is watching suspiciously to see if my brother got a bigger piece of cake than I did and feeling boiling mad about it! I have to stop myself from cutting ahead of another driver to get through the light before it changes, and if someone cuts ahead of me, I feel angry the rest of the way home. I cover it up a lot, but it's deep in there—that part of me that wants to fight."

Perhaps we can identify other central problems. Some

of us, as far back as our memories go, can remember a struggle against lethargy, inertia, something pulling back on us when we try to move ahead. We (or others) have labeled it "laziness" or "procrastination," but somehow we feel it comes from a deeper source than that.

Some of us remember always having felt a need to meddle, change things, organize things, including other people's lives, and participate in every planning session, handing out advice, feeling anxious if we are not included or elected. We have called ourselves "bossy" and "busybodies." But whatever we call it, however we laugh about it, most of our decisions and actions are based on the need to be organizing and running everything around us.

Is it a chronic loneliness we feel, a sense of always being set apart, different from others? Or is it a compulsive need to be perfect and complete in all that we think, say, and do?

Is deep, smoldering jealousy and envy our problem? Do we feel a compulsion to collect and possess things? Do we need to feel our physical bodies constantly being stimulated or nurtured through excessive eating, drinking, or sexual encounters?

Do we hate to be involved, disturbed, or challenged? Do we hate to have our comfortable way of life upset in any way and ask only of life and other people that they leave us alone?

Whatever our deep, central problem, it is an old, familiar enemy. It has been with us all our lives. It is difficult to be honest about it, because it is so old and hurtful. We are usually so ashamed of it that we try to hide it. It is frightening and humiliating to think that other people will discover this center of pain, vulnerability, and unworthiness. We devise endless masks and false fronts so others will not know what we are really like inside.

Of course, the pathetic truth is that other people usually have known all along what is our most hurtful, humiliating weakness. It shows itself in countless ways, through our habits, our mannerisms, our ways of relating, our body language. Nevertheless, only to those persons we trust the most do we dare speak of our open "secret." How do we speak of it to God? How do we pray about our most profoundly rooted problem, the blocker, the spoiler?

Many of us have simply labeled this hurting, hurtful center as sin. Was it original sin or besetting sin? It does not matter. We called it sin and asked God to take it away, to kill it, and to forgive us. We have confessed and confessed! Perhaps at some retreat we followed the suggestion of the worship leader, wrote the problem down on a slip of paper, and walked with others in ceremonial procession to a bonfire where we burned the name of our problem. For a few moments or a few days, perhaps, we felt relieved of our sin, but sooner or later it surfaced again, all the more alive and rested for its temporary eclipse.

As a next step, perhaps we looked deeper at our egos, our human identity. At this point, perhaps some author or lecturer on spiritual formation told us that we would make no progress with our central sin until we asked God to kill the ego. The *real* sin, we were told, lies not in this or that personality problem but in the very nature of our humanness, as an identity against that of God.

I have heard, and perhaps you have, that "you must break the power of the ego. You must be your own executioner. You must break through that shell of resistance and ask God to annihilate all that resists and blocks God's perfect will for you! You will make no progress until this central death to yourself is accomplished!"

This form of spiritual assault is almost as prevalent in spiritual formation circles now as in centuries past. It is not only useless; it can be extremely dangerous. To confront the human identity and its problems with violence, with the intent to break and destroy, can, and does, result in serious repression and distortion of the deep, inner human energies. This approach is all the more dangerous when a powerful surrounding group influences and encourages us in the intent to destroy parts of our selves.

When this happens, it is usually the group personality that takes over within us and dominates us; not the will of

God. Or one part of our selves, a punishing part *calling* itself God, may take over the rest of our personality, and we become more fragmented than before.

To approach ourselves and our personality problem with the wish to break and kill in the name of God is based on a deep misunderstanding of both God and ourselves. Through Jesus, we see manifested a God who is not a destroyer but a reconciler and healer, a God who desires to redeem, restore, transform all energies and all aspects of the human personality, all human communities, all aspects of the organic and inorganic universe.

> For the creation waits with eager longing for the revealing of the sons of God. . . . the creation itself will be set free from its bondage to decay and obtain the glorious liberty of the children of God.
> —Romans 8:19, 21

Healing is far more radical than destruction. Through Jesus, I do not see a God who is interested in destroying any part of us, whether the blocks, the problems, or the ego itself. I do see a God who offers to *baptize, marry, heal, and transform the ego.*

Whether our most deeply rooted problem is caused by sin or by wound, or (most likely) by a combination of the two, through Jesus we see a God who with inexorable power of compassion calls forth the innermost, most hidden self of shame, weakness, and hurt into a healed life.

This healing is possible not only because of the healing will and power of God but also because of the nature of our humanity within God.

Our energies, our powers, and our gifts came originally from the light and the hands of one Creator, who created all beings and powers in the divine image. The gift of freedom (given in some measure to all levels of creation) endowed us with the power to misuse and pervert our gifts and energies and to pass on to others, woundingly, the hurting and the hurtful.

But no matter how distorted and hurtful our powers within, they were originally created from the divine source, and they hold the potentiality for the unique and beautiful. In their healing, they are not wiped out or destroyed, for nothing in God's creation can ultimately be destroyed. Rather, they are restored to their original, intended power of gifted creativity.

Our fear, when healed, becomes intuitive, empathetic compassion and sensitivity toward others.

Our destructive anger, when healed, becomes a passion, a hunger and thirst for justice and righteousness.

Our perfectionism, our compulsion to organize and dominate, when healed, becomes released, joyous power to build and create.

Our inertia and our withdrawals, when healed, become increasing powers for peace and integrity.

Our possessiveness, our jealousies, and our physical addictions, when healed, become growing released powers to become lovers and healers of the world around us.

By asking God to kill the central block and problem, we have been asking God to kill our most divine and unique inner gift, the most living and creative part of our selves!

Slowly we learn to see our major problem not as a devil to be exorcised, a cancer to be cut out, a stumbling block to be removed, or an enemy to be killed but as our own personal "fallen angel." Or, with more poignant insight, we learn to see it as our most hurting and wounded child that hides in fear and strikes out with desperation.

This child within, the most vulnerable part of our selves, is desperately afraid. It wears and hides behind many masks: fear masquerading as anger, anger masquerading as fear. It often pretends to be a devil. It frequently pretends to be God. In fact, the part within each of us that likes to condemn, punish, humiliate, belittle, that so often pretends to be the "voice of God," is the most desperately hurt child of all.

As I write, I am looking at an old Chinese carving in ivory that I have had for a long time. It is a small piece that I can easily hold in my hand, but its significance is mighty. On one side, it is a ferociously frowning large face, utterly frightening and condemnatory. The eyes are glaring, the mouth grimly turned down. Nothing can be seen but this face of assaulting anger and judgment. But I turn the piece around, and on the other side, I see the figure of a timid, gentle, most vulnerable-looking little actor crouched down behind and speaking through the mask of the face—which is *only* a mask.

I often hold this carving and meditate on it. It has helped me immeasurably in my relation to myself and in my relation to and prayer for others. What truly lies behind the masks of angry power, the masks of cold withdrawal, the masks of busy efficiency? Do deeper fears and hurts lie behind? Does a *more* vulnerable wounded child lie beneath the one I thought I had identified in myself or in another person? What is its true name? And what, deepest of all, is its *true* unique giftedness, power, and beauty?

How can we help this child behind our masks? How can we open the door to God's full healing power to transform this most central part of our selves?

The prayer for the memories helps, certainly, up to a point. But often our basic problem seems to precede, lie deeper than our specific memories. The prayer for the subconscious certainly helps insofar as it deals with forgotten experiences that fed into and increased our basic problem.

But our deeply gifted, deeply problematic self really came into the world with us. Early wounding experiences, both remembered and forgotten, increased its hurtfulness. But the basic uniqueness of personality response was already there. All parents have noticed that within their family, one child seems, from the day of birth, to have a fighting spirit toward life. Another seems, from the first day, to shrink and withdraw. Some respond instantly and deeply to sensory stimulation. Others respond to human interaction with a mingling of communicative joy and sensitive pain. Others manifest a robust self-sufficiency, taking what they need matter-of-factly. Nurturing experiences, hurtful experiences, all are internalized and profoundly affect the human being. But the uniqueness of the potential being is already and forever present, underlying all experiences. We sense it with us always, whether in pain or joy, whether released to giftedness or bound in inward destructiveness. We sense it. We have always known it. And we can approach it consciously and directly through prayer.

Suggested Prayer: *Prayer for the Inner Child*

Relax your body, and give thanks to God that the divine love is always present, always embracing you. Think of such verses as: "By this we shall know that we are of the truth, and reassure our hearts before him whenever our hearts condemn us; for God is greater than our hearts, and he knows everything" (1 John 3:19–20).

Picture Jesus Christ (in whatever form the love of God through Christ best comes to you) entering the room and filling it with warmth and comfort. He who said, "Let the children come to me" (Luke 18:16), now tenderly calls forth your own most deeply wounded, problematic self.

The one you have hidden, the one you have hated, the one within who feels the weakest, the ugliest, the most vulnerable, the most shameful, the frightening or the most frightened comes forward—like a hurt child. (Some people see it as a little animal, a shrub, and so on.) Together, you and Jesus look on it compassionately. Look at the expression in its face, and listen to what it is trying to say in its own words. You need not fear it, because the love of God in Jesus is with you.

Embrace your "child" if you can, but do not force yourself to do this if you don't want to touch it. Later this reluctance will also be healed. Say to it: "I hear you. I didn't realize how badly you were hurting. You belong to me, but I can't heal you alone. Let's go together to the One who *can* heal."

Now release your inner child to Jesus' healing hands. If

you find that for some reason you cannot do this or that your inner hurt self does not want to go to those hands, *do not force the release*. Ask Jesus to come to you both, putting his arms around both you and your inner child. But if you can, image Jesus taking your inner child fully into his hands and arms, into the light, into the central heart of love, and holding it there.

Sit quietly, giving thanks that this deep, central, hurting part of yourself is now being deeply held, comforted, healed, restored slowly to its original beauty and unique creativity.

After a while, it will seem that the child is being restored to you. Or you may, instead, image it still being carried in the divine heart of transforming love.

Give thanks, breathe deeply of God's breath of life, and conclude the prayer, perhaps with the biblical passage:

That you, being rooted and grounded in love, may have power to comprehend . . . what is the breadth and length and height and depth, and to know the love of Christ which surpasses knowledge, that you may be filled with all the fulness of God.
—Ephesians 3:17–19

It is important in this prayer, whether experienced individually or in a group situation, not to force any images. Let God's love come to you in whatever way is best and most spontaneous to you. Let your inner child come forth in whatever way seems natural. Let the willingness to fully release the child come slowly if it needs to. You should not ride roughshod over your inner resistances. Resistances are there for a reason. You have probably built up deep defenses because of hurtful experiences, and these defenses held you together when you needed some such support. Now that God's love through Christ is becoming fully revealed in your life, you will slowly lower the defenses through healing of memories and growing trust. But this will take some time. Never forcibly assault your inner defenses, and *never allow anyone else to do so!* That is not the way the Holy Spirit works. And those who come to you truly through the Holy Spirit will not assault your defenses. God through Christ respects and has compassion on your inner defenses. They will be healed, you will outgrow them, but within the timing and context of God's grace.

You will probably need, many times, to return your inner child to the healing hands of God through Christ. It is your central gifted power and has probably been wounded a long time. But slowly its original and powerful meaning and its true face of creative beauty will be revealed to you as God's work of integration and healing deepens within you.

CHAPTER SEVEN

Prayer for the Hurts of the World

Just as the healed healthy body gets up, stretches, and moves, so does the human personality healed by God long to be involved in loving, creative encounter with other human beings. Reaching out to heal others is a spontaneous development in the growing wholeness of our spirits. Just as the yeast kneaded into the dough acts, grows, and manifests itself throughout the changing loaf, so does the radical act of God within us work change *in* us and *through* us. This change is that of passion and compassion as we encounter the agony of the torn, fragmented world around us.

Within a few months after consenting to God's deep healing within myself, I began to notice a new, painful awareness of the hurting people around me. On buses, in airports, on the busy sidewalks of the city I began to notice faces lined with pain and weariness. It became painful to open the newspaper and to watch the evening news. As the healing deepened within me, the sensitivity grew. I began to want to *do* something for the wounds of others. I began to realize that this longing was an inseparable part of growing within the healing of God's love.

Many people fear that if they take the time and energy to respond in depth to God's love through prayer they will start withdrawing from the world, its people, its pain. In every retreat and workshop I lead, the participants always raise this question with great anxiety. They worry that the adventure of the inner healing will make them escapists, detached and indifferent to compassionate responsibility.

"What right do I have to think about my own inner

needs and hurts and to ask God to heal them, when one-fourth of the world's population goes to sleep hungry every night?" one young minister demanded in passionate sincerity.

"Are we justified in courses on inner healing and prayer when the world is in danger of atomic holocaust and extinction?" a young woman theological student asked recently. "Is *any* prayer relevant any more except, 'Lord have mercy'?"

These are honest and important questions, which need to be asked. Two thoughts occur to me as I encounter these challenges.

First, depth healing prayer not only raises our inner awareness of the pain of the world, but it is also a direct action *in* the world. Prayer does not merely inspire us to action; it *is* action. A great spiritual leader once said that the praying person is releasing new healing energy into the very life stream, just as a living plant is releasing oxygen into the atmosphere.

In depth prayer we change, and the situation around us changes, far beyond what we can measure. The word *retreat* is the wrong word to describe what happens when a group of praying men and women meet together in the act of channeling God's healing into the world. There is no retreat going on. It is an *advance*. It is the very frontier of God's creativity encountering chaos.

Secondly, I learned in my years as pastor in a large city that the effort to face human suffering and injustice without a vital life of prayer and inner healing can (and does) lead to a vicious circle of exhaustion, anger, and judgmental manipulation of others. We cannot change ourselves and others depending on only our own good intentions, our ability to love, our willpower. As I stressed in the first chapter, if we try to extend the outer branches of fruitful action without deepening the roots of dependence on God's nurture, we move quickly into serious fatigue and even burnout. When that happens, some individuals experience a breakdown. Some individuals feel increasing anger, and they manipulate others as a result of their own fatigue and unhealed wounds. Most ministers and active lay leaders learn this sooner or later—often the hard way.

Rather than entering the vicious circle of unnurtured, unhealed action, fatigue, and judgmental anger, we are instead called to the cycle of grace: inner healing, compassionate awareness of others, healing action, and then *deeper* inner nurture and healing.

God has never asked us to work on the frontier of redemptive action within the world in an unhealed, unnurtured, self-dependent condition. With mingled joy and pain we will discover, as I described at the beginning of this chapter, that the longing to reach out with healing becomes one of the firstfruits of a healthy individual and community.

How can we best pray for others? How can we most fully cooperate with God's redemptive, healing will in this world through prayer?

First, I think we need to look at our attitudes toward and our interpretation of intercessory prayer. What are we really doing? What do we think is happening? What do we believe God wills and does?

Prayer for others is basically the same as the depth healing prayer we are learning to pray for ourselves. The prayer for our own inner children, whether of memory or personality problem, is excellent practice for prayer for the other person. It is based on the faith that God longs, far more than we do, for the wholeness and healing of every part of the universe, every person in the world. When we pray for others as for ourselves, we are not begging or pleading with God to do something. We are not urging a reluctant Creator to act in mercy. God *is* mercy. God *is* love. God is already completely and forever on the side of all that reconciles, redeems, heals, and makes whole in life. This we are told repeatedly throughout the New Testament. When we pray, "Lord, hear our prayer" or "Spare us, Lord," we insult and demean God who has already told us that the divine nature and name is love and that the divine consciousness always hears us, even before we speak. God is not deaf, reluctant, or merciless. God does not hide from our need. So why do we pray as if that was the case?

Rather, in our praying, let us realize that God was already way ahead of us in the divine-human encounter, already with us, already around and within us, already knocking on our closed doors and speaking and calling to us before we thought to pray in response.

Prayer is our response to the God who has already and has forever spoken to us. Prayer is our response to the embrace that has forever surrounded us. Prayer is our response to the comfort, healing, and transformation forever offered to us.

Second, in our prayer for others it is supremely important to realize that it is not our willpower and love healing others but the love of God channeled through us. Nothing can exhaust us more quickly than attempting to heal others through our own strength. Prayer is not a generative action; it is a transmissive action. If we forget to pray, act, and move through the nurturing power of God's life only, not only can we become extremely exhausted, but we can actually internalize the wounds and the symptoms of others.

A third vital point to remember is that it is not up to us either to diagnose or to prescribe. We cannot know the source of the other person's problem and wound, and we cannot know at what level and in what way the healing may best begin. It is presumptuous and limiting to try to make these decisions. Intercessory prayer groups have often earned a bad reputation because of their diagnosing and prescribing.

"Obviously John's problems are due to his smoking habit," one group may decide. "Therefore, we will all concentrate in prayer to make him stop smoking!" There is no question but that the concentration of a group has great power. But how does such a group presume to know that the smoking habit is the most basic problem? What if the desire to smoke arose from a deeper need and deprivation? If the deeper need is not met, will John start some more dangerous habit when he stops smoking?

"Let's all join in prayer that Ann will join a church, get

a good job, and find a nice husband," another group may decide. How do they know that Ann can cope with church, better job, and nice husband? How do they know but that healing and transformation need to begin on another level and work first in very different parts of her life and personality?

Misused prayer can quickly become a kind of interference, manipulation, and even brainwashing of another person. It is far more holistic and trustful of God to release the whole person for whom we pray into the healing hands, into the healing light. And as we release, we offer ourselves as channels that God's healing power may be thus focused and intensified in the other person's life.

A serious question usually arises at this point. Will something really happen? Why do so many prayers seem to be unanswered? There is no easy answer. Certainly we do not believe it is God's will that anyone live a life of fragmentation and suffering and unhealed wounds, whether inner or outer. That is not the God we see through Jesus whose whole ministry was concerned with healing inner and outer pain. Why then so many blocks?

Is it the lack of faith? Even that is not an adequate answer when we see how many believers seem to experience such obstacles to healing.

My only answer (and it is a very limited one) is that though God has no limits of love and desire to heal us, nevertheless God has chosen to work through our awakened and compassionate channeling consciousness. This may be a form of divine self-limitation. God waits for our consent, not just the individual consent but the *community* consent and openness. God is concerned with the awakening and sensitization of all our human consciousness on every level. If we live, move, and have our being in communities whose mind-set is permeated with fear of God, ignorance of God's love and power to heal, and denial of the power of prayer, it is probably difficult for full healing power to be experienced. In a similar way, as we saw in the chapter on nurturing prayer, it is difficult to experience the full, releasing, nurturing power of God's light in our bodies if we are tightened up, defensive, or closed off. A human community is rather like a body. If it is open, relaxed, and expectant, transforming miracles can happen. If it is tight and resistant, though God's love is there forever, the healing is blocked and delayed. Blocks, defenses, and resistances probably exist on many levels, as we saw in our prayer for the subconscious.

This point is most important. Many people feel *personally* guilty when healing seems delayed, and they wonder if they have failed in trust of God. It may not be the case at all. They are probably sharing deeply the unhealed inner wounds and blocks of their human communities and also the struggles in the realm of nature itself which still groans and travails (Rom. 8:22). Let us release one another from these burdens of undeserved guilt. But let us also pray unceasingly for the *inner* healing, at depth, for one another and our communities so that inner fears and resistances may be healed, our defensive doors opened, our communities and nature itself set free in the "glorious liberty of the children of God" (Rom. 8:21).

In addition to releasing the person for whom we pray to God's light, it is extremely helpful to picture the wounded child within the other held in Christ's healing hands. This is a prayer I have found to be helpful for my inner self and it is no less helpful for another.

This is not the same as trying to diagnose another person's problem. But if we are troubled by another person's fear, anger, loneliness, or aggression, we can try to visualize the hurting, vulnerable child hiding beneath the surface. We admit we cannot know the actual problem. Only God knows what that is. But we can pray for other people as they seem to come across to us.

For example, I found myself becoming extremely annoyed by a certain woman's uptight, repressive, rather judgmental manner. Every time I saw her I got more irritated. The expression on her face, the set of her mouth, the way she sat in her chair, the impatient way she tapped her foot, the sharp tone of her voice, all maddened me. (Incidentally, when we feel this way about another person, it can be most enlightening to ask ourselves if there is something in the person that reminds us of ourselves.) Prayer did not seem to help at all. I still couldn't stand her. Then one day, while I was crossly thinking about her, it suddenly occurred to me that underneath the repressive, rigid manner was probably a very sensitive little girl who all her life had been trying to do and say and be exactly the right thing. The little girl was trying very hard to win the approval and respect of others. The little girl swallowed down her hurts and tried to be brave and strong. Perhaps it was a little girl that she, this woman, did not know about anymore.

What a difference! After that, I prayed for that little girl. When I met the woman, I seemed to see the sensitive child close behind the face of the stern adult. I found myself relating differently to her. I found myself feeling differently about her. I seemed to sense a change in her response to me. We have not become best friends (not yet), but we have a warmth and growing openness now where before were only cold dislike and defensiveness.

Is it presumptuous to pray for the little girl I seemed to sense within her? I think not, because I did not try to diagnose the real problem of the child within nor was I telling God what should be done about her. Rather, I reminded myself that God already completely loved and understood her, and I offered myself as channel so that the full power of healing might be made manifest in her life. Then I pictured the sensitive child within her, released to the healing hands of Christ, held in those arms, able at last to relax the defenses and to rest on the perfect love that enfolded her.

Perhaps more significantly, I found that thus praying, some of my *own* defenses and immaturities were being healed. We are not just lifeless channels when we pray for others. In God's divine ecology we too are being helped and healed. Perhaps this is the reason for God's choosing to heal us, transform us, through the openness of the human concern, one to another.

We can pray for one another's memories, just as we are learning to pray for our own. An elderly man once told me that one of his earliest memories of himself was his hugging the legs of his father, longing to be picked up and embraced, and feeling lonely and bereft when it didn't happen. When I prayed for him later, I pictured that little boy still within him being willing to be picked up by God's own loving power, comforted and healed of that bereftness.

Can such prayers be helpful if the persons are not praying those prayers for themselves? Can such prayers help them even if they do not know we are praying for them? It is true that the other person always has free will and is permitted to close the inner doors to God's healing. Prayer for another never negates the free decision of the other person. God's Holy Spirit always respects the decision and the free consent. But often there is, beneath the surface, an unexpressed longing to be helped. Often an inner readiness lies far below the apparent surface resistance, and the time is right to respond fully to God's love. In this case, the prayer of healing offered up for that person is helpful in ways we cannot yet imagine or measure.

Can we pray for our communities in a similar way? In recent months I have been thinking a great deal about this and have come to believe that not only *can* we thus pray for our communities, but we *must*, in some form, pray for the deep hurt of every community "soul," or our world will not experience healing.

I first began to think seriously about this form of prayer when I was asked to lead a retreat for a church that had recently lost its pastor under circumstances agonizingly traumatic for both pastor and people. As I sat with the group of lay leaders in the church parlor and we talked and prayed together, I became aware that I was not sitting with just a group of hurting bewildered *individuals*. It was as if the group there had a personality, a soul of its own, that was wounded. I shared my impression, and we began to pray for the wounded memory of the group, as if the group were one person.

Since then, I have thought what a change there would be in this world if we, as individuals and groups, would pray for the deeply buried pain and forgotten griefs of the groups to which we belong: family, church, nation, race, sex, profession. Who can doubt that each family has its own special soul and that all members of the family through the generations are affected for good or ill by the gifts, powers, and wounds of that unique family spirit?

Don't we experience the same thing in our churches, our denominations? Wounds are passed on through the decades, and all who come within the encompassing spirit of each church are influenced by the unhealed pain it bears and empowered by its special gift and charism.

Certainly in the smoldering, resentful feuds and savage wars between races and nations we seem to see the wounded, unhealed group souls striking out in pain against one another. And individual members, often without memory or specific knowledge of the generations of the burden of the pain, are drawn into the wrath and conflict. Even as a child, I was haunted by Matthew Arnold's poignant vision in his tragic poem "Dover Beach":

> And we are here as on a darkling plain
> Swept with confused alarms of struggle and flight,
> Where ignorant armies clash by night.

Our "ignorant armies" for centuries have been acting and reacting to levels of pain, barely understood, that have sunk long ago into the subconscious souls of the nations.

What would happen if a group within each family began to pray for the wounded soul of that family?

What would happen if each church had a small group within it that opened channels for healing at the very roots of its early pain?

What if groups of women began to pray for the hurts the spirit of womankind had received through the centuries?

What if groups of men began to pray for the wounds thrust upon the spirit of mankind?

What if groups within all races did the same? Denominations within the churches? Nations? Schools? Neighborhoods?

What could be a form of such intercessory prayer for our communities? Perhaps we could visualize the deep wounded spirit of each community the way we visualize it for ourselves or another individual: as a desperately hurt and hurting child, who has great potentiality for creative power and giftedness, released to the healing, transforming hands of the Christ. Or we could use the form of prayer suggested in the prayer for the subconscious self in chapter four.

Suggested Prayer One: *Prayer for Hurts of the World*

This prayer can be used by an individual or a group. If you are praying in a group, agree on what community will be prayed for. Relax your body, breathe gently the breath of life from God. Give thanks that the love of God completely surrounds and protects you. Visualize the Christ present with you in the room.

Give your consent to walk with the Christ to the entrance to the deeply rooted pain of your group. Do not try to evoke details or old wrongs. Simply walk with Christ to the entrance where they lie buried. Think of the witness of power in Romans 8:

> Who shall separate us from the love of Christ? Shall tribulation, or distress, or persecution, or famine, or nakedness, or peril, or sword? . . . No, in all these things we are more than conquerors through him who loved us.
>
> —Romans 8:35, 37

Ask the Christ to open the door to that entrance and to enter the depths of your group pain with the full power of healing light. *Do not try to enter also.* Do not try to see the depths that the Christ sees and touches. Stand outside the entrance, offering yourself as the channel for the intensification of this healing process. Do not strain for any special feeling or make any special effort of willpower. It is God through Christ who is the healer, not you.

Affirm in faith that empowered healing is now moving and changing at the depths of the group you represent. Give thanks that the unique gift and beauty of your group is bit by bit being released. Ask the Christ to put his own special protection on that entrance. When it seems right, conclude your prayer with thanksgiving.

> For I am sure that neither death, nor life, nor angels, nor principalities, nor things present, nor things to come, nor powers, nor height, nor depth, nor anything else in all creation, will be able to separate us from the love of God in Christ Jesus our Lord.
>
> —Romans 8:38–39

A depth prayer for the wound of a group soul is best experienced in a group situation, with mutual support, nurture, and channeling.

These suggestions are just some of the alternative ways in which God calls us to work on the frontiers of the world's pain. It is profoundly redemptive to pray, also in a group context, for the world itself. A prayer for the world can be similar to the prayer of the heart discussed in the second chapter. The globe of the world can be visualized with the glowing light of Christ at its very center.

Suggested Prayer Two: *Prayer for Globe of the World*

Place your crossed palms over your heart area, central in your chest, and relax your body. Visualize the world itself held in the hands of Christ and the transforming light radiating from the earth's heart—just as you have pictured your human body.

Slowly say: "The living heart of Jesus Christ is taking form within this world, filling it . . . calming it . . . healing it . . . restoring it . . . bringing new life. And this transformed life flows peacefully, with full healing power . . . into every continent . . . every ocean . . . every nation (with your hands opened), and we give thanks to God that this healing is taking place."

Rest quietly, holding the inner picture of the earth's body glowing and permeated with the divine light. Bring the prayer to a gentle end.

You might wish to read the great cosmic hymn in Colossians: "He has delivered us from the dominion of darkness and transferred us to the kingdom of his beloved Son, in whom we have redemption. . . . He is before all things, and in him all things hold together" (Col. 1:13–14, 17).

"Lord, make me an instrument of your peace," Saint Francis prayed long ago. We are just beginning to learn ways by which God calls us into the redemptive activity of prayer. We learn and grow in the awe of deepening love, knowing that every prayer offered in sincerity and loving concern brings closer the day when "the earth shall be full of the knowledge of the Lord/as the waters cover the sea" (Isa. 11:9).

CHAPTER EIGHT

Prayer through the Stressful Day

How can we, as individuals and groups, bring into our full and stressful days some of these concepts of healing, transforming prayer?

Obviously, every day we can't move through the prayer for the wounded memories back to babyhood. It isn't likely that with clocklike regularity we will pray for the subconscious self, the hurting roots of some community, or the heart of the world. Nor every day will we have long periods for soaking prayer.

Nor should we try! As emphasized in the second chapter, prayer is ultimately a relationship, not a daily discipline to be approached in the same way, at the same time, for the same length of time every day. All living relationships, though they give rise to their own dependable rhythm, are flexible, open-ended. The methodologies that rise out of a living, healthy relationship will change, grow, and evolve even as the relationship itself grows deeper.

Somehow we have internalized certain fixed ideas about the ways we ought to pray, and these rigid mystiques can do much harm if we are trying to force ourselves into a pattern that is not right for us or that violates our own inner growth pattern and timing. For example, it was years before I really consented to the thought that two o'clock in the afternoon is as holy a time as six in the morning and that God is as much present!

I had always taken for granted that a truly prayerful person who really put God first would, of course, get in at least an hour of prayer before breakfast. What a shock, what a relief, when I discovered that God loves and responds to us "afternoon types" every bit as much!

"But the morning is so peaceful and still," the traditionalist will argue. "One can encounter God so much more clearly and deeply before the world wakes up and the work of the day begins."

For years I consented guiltily to this idea. But in recent years I have learned enough about God and myself to be able to reply cheerfully: "That may be true for *you*, and I am happy for you. But it is definitely not true for *me*. It has never been true for me. I think lovingly of God and speak to God briefly when I first awake, but my deepest encounter comes several hours later when the work of the day is half over. Early afternoon is when I find myself most rested, most alert, most sensitively attuned to the voice of God within."

The point is, our methodology of prayer should rise with grace and naturalness out of the uniqueness of relationship we each have with God. Here are some suggested discerning points about the wholeness and appropriateness of our methodologies in prayer.

First, does our prayer method allow for God's grace? Or have we imposed rigid structures and patterns on ourselves? God's approach to us is custom-made, not assembly line output. Often there are surprises; always there is freshness.

Second, does our chosen method of prayer take into consideration our basic type of personality? Some of us are ordered, regular, rather structured types, and others are much more spontaneous, nonstructured types. Some people find it natural and comfortable to designate a certain time and place every day for prayer time, whereas others find that confining and prefer an ongoing dialogue through the day. That is the way these types best relate to other people, and that is the way they feel they best relate to God. Whatever type we are, we should affirm ourselves and others and know that God loves and respects our type of personality.

Third, our prayer method should take into account our personal needs and timing. As indicated in chapter two, we cannot always approach God in the liturgical order of adoration, confession, petition, intercession, thanksgiving, and commitment. At some time during the day (or the week) it is healthy to move into these various areas of deep relatedness to God, but if our relationship with God is to become healthy, holistic, vital, and natural, we must feel free to communicate with God spontaneously on *any* level of need and thought. It does not matter that it may be childish or unworthy. It does not matter that it may be material rather than spiritual. It does not matter that it may be trivial rather than important. It does not matter that it may seem selfish. *What matters is that we have approached God freely and honestly.*

When men, women, and children came to Jesus with their needs and concerns—hunger, illness, problems in the family—he did not tell them to stop thinking about themselves and get their minds on higher things. He did not rebuke them for thinking about the needs of the body instead of the soul. He met people where they were. He fed them, healed them, and encountered them fully and compassionately. And as we are encountered with full compassion by God at whatever point we are, we are nurtured and released to grow more deeply into maturity.

Fourth, our prayer method should not demand or program certain types of response or experience. Many people are troubled because they do not seem to have the mystical experiences that others do. Others are worried because they do not receive guidance in the way their friends receive it. Perhaps they do not have inner visualizations in prayer. Perhaps they do not experience physical healing as quickly as others. They do not have the types of emotional response that seem to be expected. They feel left out, left behind, somehow lacking because their experiences are different.

It is important to realize that we each are unique, like snowflakes or fingerprints. God does not program prescribed responses from us, so neither should our prayer method or our prayer group be programmed.

If the dissimilarity and pressure seem really pronounced and uncomfortable, that may indicate we are in a group or a community really not right or natural for us. It may be a sign that we should seek a different kind of fellowship.

Fifth, if, on the other hand, *nothing* is happening to us or in us as a result of our prayer method or our prayer group, it may be a sign that we do need an approach to God more stimulating and challenging than we have allowed ourselves. "God is not a mush of concession," as Emerson expressed it. When we have opened ourselves at depth to God's compassionate but also radical transformation within, something always happens within us. There is always some change on some level: a change in the understanding of the self, a change in health, a change in relationships, a change in habits, a change in compassionate and moral awareness. If there has been no change in us whatever after several months with a certain prayer method (it is wise to check this out with a trusted friend), we may well need more challenge.

Sixth, whatever our prayer method, we should remember there are seasons of the spirit. There are times in our spiritual formation (as in any aspect of our lives) when we feel energetic and outwardly expressive, and there are times when we feel inward and quiescent. There are times when we feel deeply emotionally responsive to God and rapidly changing within, and there are times when we feel cool and emotionless. We take these changes for granted at different times of the day or the year ("I always feel unresponsive in the morning" or "January and February are my slack times"), but we are troubled when we find our relationship with God sometimes low-key, unemotional, quiescent, or even tired.

Such times do not necessarily mean that we have fallen away from God or that something is wrong with our way of praying. It usually means that we are experiencing the nor-

mal ups and downs, the emotional ins and outs of any relationship or project. Often these quiescent times can be
extremely creative and helpful if we don't try to force ourselves out of them. These may be times in which some deep
healing or new growth is being experienced at levels far below our consciousness. (I believe it is when the mother bear
is deeply somnolent in her hibernation period that the bear
cubs are born!) Fallow periods are healthy for all of us.

Of course, if the fatigue, the distancing is extreme, or if
it is experienced for unusually long periods, it may be a sign
that we are tired or being drained for reasons other than that
of our usual cycle and that we need to look at the stress and
conflict in our lives. We may need for a while to move into a
time of nurturing and restorative prayer as described in
chapter two.

What are some ways—ways that affirm our humanness, ways that take into account our timing and the type of
person we are, ways that deepen our closeness with God and
cooperate with God in the healing, transforming work
within us and through us—by which we can pray through a
busy day?

The following suggestions are ways I have found myself
to be helped in my growing. But each person must feel free
to allow many changes in imagery, timing, and approach
according to the guiding of God's spirit within.

One Method of Daily Prayer

Waking: Though you are drowsy and unclear, gently and
consciously for a few moments breathe each breath as God's
own breath of life breathed into you. Image God's regenerating light (perhaps in gold or rose color) flowing around your
body and into it. Rest in the light. You may wish to pray the
prayer of the heart described in chapter two. If the memory
of a dream surfaces naturally, ask if it has any symbolic significance for you but do not force any memory or intepreta-
tion.

You may wish to gently and briefly massage your hands, arms, face, greeting your body with loving nurture as it begins the day. You may wish to think of some verses of praise and restoration such as Psalm 63: "O God, thou art my God, I seek thee, my soul thirsts for thee; my flesh faints for thee. . . . Because thy steadfast love is better than life, my lips will praise thee" (Psalm 63:1, 3).

Cleansing and Dressing: As you wash in running water, try to think of the water as symbolic of (and also channeling) God's cleansing and refreshing action in you. Let the water become a sacramental way by which God's real presence touches you.

If your mind is foggy in the early morning, you may be helped by having a short prayer, a Bible verse, or a helpful picture on your mirror or wall to read or think about while you dress. Don't force any special feeling or emotional response. Just reading the words or looking at the picture with consent and openness helps you in a very real way. The verse that I love especially at the beginning of the day, that I have taped on my wall to read while preparing for the day ahead, is the promise to God's people: "For you shall go out in joy, and be led forth in peace; the mountains and the hills before you shall break forth into singing" (Isa. 55:12).

Facing the Day: If possible, before or during breakfast take a few moments to think over tasks and experiences that lie ahead for the day. Claim God's promise that the divine love and light will go before you. Visualize Christ already at your place of work, filling it with light, healing and transforming the experiences to come.

This can be prayed while walking, driving, or riding on the bus as well as while sitting in stillness.

In the Midst of the Day: As you approach a stressful task, find yourself in the midst of a stress or a problem, or have a few minutes' break, visualize the healing light flowing around your body and into all parts of your body. Visualize the field of light enfolding you like a cloak.

Relax your muscles, breathe gently, get in touch with

your feelings. With compassion embrace these feelings like inner children. Try to release them into Christ's hands.

In Relationships: As you encounter other people during the day, whether face-to-face or by letter or phone, visualize the light of God surrounding each one. (This is especially helpful in committee meetings.) Ask God to help you become compassionately aware of the hurt, frightened, lonely, or bewildered child in the other person and visualize that part embraced by Christ. Also, try to become aware of the special, unique beauty and giftedness in the other person, and pray in thankfulness for it.

Thankful Openness: At some moment in the day, deliberately gaze at a tree, a shrub, a flower, a bird, a cloud, sunlight, rain, and greet it as a loving partner. Look at it fully and lovingly. Touch it if you can or open your palms to its presence. Let God's love speak, reach out to you through it. Move gently deeper than the outward appearance and greet the hidden, living mystery.

This sacramental encounter need not be only through sight. We can just as fully greet God's love through a sound, a fragrance, a taste, or a touch.

At Bedtime: Relax your body, quietly breathe the breath of life from God. Again visualize the relaxing, nurturing light flowing through your body.

Some biblical verses of deep peace may come to mind, such as:

> My mouth praises thee with joyful lips,
> when I think of thee upon my bed,
>   and meditate on thee in the watches of the night;
> for thou hast been my help,
>   and in the shadow of thy wings
>   I sing for joy.
> My soul clings to thee;
>   thy right hand upholds me.
>
> —Psalm 63:5–8

> In peace I will both lie down and sleep;
>   for thou alone, O Lord, makest me dwell in safety.
> —Psalm 4:8

Think over some of the experiences of the day, perhaps only two or three of them. Place these experiences in Christ's healing hands. Think of one or two persons you have met who are in special need. Release them to the healing hands. Think of some special beautiful thing, some special help or joy you experienced, and smile at God with loving thanks. Listen for some inner motion of God's guidance.

Think of the restful sleep to come as a chance for the deeper release and adventure of the spirit while the body and the emotional consciousness enter the nurturing rest. As Brother Lawrence said in *Practicing the Presence of God:* "Those who have the wind of the Holy Spirit, go forward even in sleep."

If you wake in the night in restlessness, see if there is any special problem or hurt you have overlooked that needs to be put in the hands of Christ. Then, with your hands crossed on your heart, move in a relaxed way through the prayer of the heart (see chapter two).

Being human, you will probably not touch on all these frontiers of prayer every day. On some days or even for some weeks, you will perhaps move through only one or two of these encounter places of prayer. At other periods in life, you will find yourself longing to experience all these encounter points each day. Listen to your inner guidance and needs.

Some of these encounters with God may be for only a few seconds. You may expand others into half-hour sessions. You may be the type who wishes and is able to schedule a long session of such praying into each day. Or you may be the type who sits down to pray the prayers of inner depth healing and transformation only once or twice a week and prays through the average day in a kind of ongoing awareness of God. The suggested method just outlined is only a framework with spaces for an infinite variety of responses to the divine relationship that embraces us.

CHAPTER NINE

The Adventure of the Transformed Self

When we have allowed God's healing light to enter us fully, there is a change within us. Some of these changes come slowly, others swiftly. Some may come almost simultaneously, whereas others may come during long-spaced intervals. We cannot tell in which order the changes will come. Sometimes we will be immediately conscious of inner changes, and at other times we may be aware of nothing happening on the surface but great transformation may be occurring at levels far below the conscious awareness.

In George MacDonald's *Anthology,* this point is effectively stated:

> To give us the spiritual gift we desire, God may have to begin far back in our spirit, in regions unknown to us, and do much work that we can be aware of only in the results; for our consciousness is to the extent of our being but as the flame of the volcano to the world-gulf whence it issues. In the gulf of our unknown being God works behind our consciousness. With His holy influence, with His own presence, (the one thing for which we most earnestly cry) He may be approaching our consciousness from behind, coming forward through regions of our darkness into our light, long before we begin to be aware that He is answering our request—has answered it, and is visiting His child.

Eventually we will realize that the divine yeast is truly at work within us and that we are changing in ways we had not dreamed. Oddly enough, these inner changes which begin to seem so powerful do not seem to make us strange to ourselves. Instead we seem to be at last truly finding ourselves, coming home to our real selves at last. There is a feeling of rightness, inevitability, and authenticity about these changes. Though surprising, they seem completely natural.

One of the first changes we notice is a strengthening of the sense of identity, a more powerful *self*. This is not to be confused with selfishness. Selfish persons usually lack a strong sense of central identity. Because those persons are so empty or unawakened within, they need to grasp possessively at outer things and to respond self-centeredly in every situation. It is a reaction based on fear and inner emptiness. When persons who have no rich, true inner identity merge with a political party, a cultural community, a cause, a platform, a grievance, or a spirit of revenge *as* their identity, a potentially dangerous situation results. The anger, the loneliness, the fear, and the vengeance become the central ego of the person, and the person swiftly becomes a manipulator or the victim of a manipulator.

"The glory of God is the fully alive human being," wrote the second-century church father Irenaeus. What a magnificent vision of God's will and longing for us! To enter into the full life of God, the full relationship with God, we individuals need a healed, whole self, a healthy identity with which to relate to God and to the world. As explained in chapter six, God does not break down the ego, the self. God marries it. God heals and transforms it.

Along with this growing awareness of the reality and beauty of our identity comes a growing awareness of the identity of others. We begin to see other people not just as means to our ends, not just as annoying blocks or helping hands, not just as types, cases, or categories, but as unique creations. We begin to see the hurts and wounds within them as wounded children. We begin to see their giftedness, their beauty, their loneliness, and their longing (perhaps deeply frustrated) to reach out to others. We sense within our selves, as our own healing grows within us, a desire to reach out in compassion and communication.

We notice a change in response to the physical world

around us, including our own bodies, especially after the restorative experiences of soaking prayer and the prayer of the heart. Our bodies become trusted friends and partners rather than enemies, deadweights, or spoiled, demanding children. We receive increasingly the nurture of God through *all* our senses of sight, hearing, touch, taste, and smell. Instead of being too physical, those who feel compulsive in their eating, drinking, or sexual encounters are probably not being physical enough. Instead of receiving God's renewing reenergizing through the full spectrum of the five senses, they are receiving energy through only one or two. They are in a state of sensory starvation. As we become more open and receptive to the sensory world around us, the things we see, hear, taste, touch, and smell become more precious and keenly valued, but we become less compulsive and possessive about them. As every bite of food becomes sacramental, we do not need to eat so much. As we become increasingly aware of the preciousness of animals, plants, water, and air, we become less arrogant and complacent in our use of them and grow into more reverence, gentleness, and responsibility for their well-being. As other people become dear to us and valued as ends in themselves, we are less tempted to manipulate or misuse them sexually. As we are deeply healed and made whole, we are increasingly released to see and to touch all things like lovers!

Does that mean that as we grow, we will no longer eat meat or swat flies or pull up weeds? Not yet, probably. We are not at that place yet in our evolving spirituality in this world. It does mean that we pull the weed or kill the fly no longer with the callous attitude, "You have no right to exist," but rather with some sorrow that we have not yet, as human beings, learned to exist in this world without some kind of destruction. Also, we will be enabled to do what we feel we must do for survival with the hope and faith that the day will come which God has promised, the day when, as it is written in Isaiah:

> They shall not hurt or destroy in all my holy mountain;
> for the earth shall be full of the knowledge of the Lord
>   as the waters cover the sea.
>   —Isaiah 11:9

In the meantime, as we grow into becoming channels of that promised time, we can touch, take, and eat with reverence and gratitude the bodies of animals and plants, and we can learn ways to protest and prevent all needless suffering of all living things.

This new, responsible awareness becomes a growing *moral* awareness. The healed, revitalized personality begins to discern change in values, change in priorities, change in choices, change in attitudes and decisions.

We do not need to use force on the inner self as it grows into new answers, new moral decisions, but rather we become sensitively alert to a developing inner sense of rightness and wrongness. I have found a special form of prayer extraordinarily helpful when I am perplexed about a moral decision or direction for myself. I call it "the radical prayer":

> *Holy Spirit, if this is right for me, let it become more firmly rooted and established in my life. If this is wrong for me, let it become less important to me, and let it be increasingly removed from my life.*

We should not pray this prayer unless we mean it. It is always heard and answered in definite and surprising ways. Habits begin to lose their grip. Relationships change. Neglected parts of our selves begin to grow. New attractions and likings surface. Surprising abilities appear. Some familiar old tendencies become unattractive to us. Something always happens when we pray this prayer in honesty.

One woman, uncertain if her strong, persistent, and growing interest in making money was becoming an immoral compulsion, prayed this prayer in sincerity and awaited results. Within a few weeks her attention was directed toward a new line of work in which she was much more interested in the creative activity than in the salary. She still has a healthy interest in a reasonable salary, but it is no longer the compulsive center of her life.

A young man, puzzled over the nature of his strong attraction to an older, married woman, prayed this prayer, and as the weeks passed he discovered the overwhelming attraction was turning into a calm friendship with a constant lessening of the compulsive need to be with the woman.

An older man, unsure of God's guidance about the use of his time, prayed the radical prayer, and in a short time he found some old interests decreasing and new concerns and enthusiasms rapidly growing.

Does this mean we can judge God's guidance in our lives merely by our likes and dislikes? That, of course, would be far too simplistic. But if by such a radical prayer prayed in honesty we put ourselves deliberately under God's guidance and thus release ourselves to God's direction, our changing feelings and reactions become increasingly significant and indicative of change within.

Augustine said, "Love God, and do as you like." That sounds dangerous until we realize that by the deepening love and relationship with God, we are so changed that what pleases us is the very thing God had wanted for us all along. It is by the resulting fruits in our lives that we can best discern God's guidance, of course.

Do we feel a growing sense of inner freedom in our choices and attitudes? God's spirit releases us from compulsion of all kinds.

Do we feel a growing joy in our lives, in spite of difficulties, challenges, or pain? A life with decreasing joy (no matter how righteous) is a sign that something has gone wrong.

Is compassion growing in our lives toward both ourselves and others? It is a danger signal if we feel increasing judgment, contempt, or distancing.

Do we feel a growing sense of authenticity, meaningfulness in our lives, with increasing naturalness and spontaneity? A sense of homecoming in our decisions and actions?

Do we feel strength given for our tasks and resulting fruitfulness? If we feel constantly weak, uninspired, unenthusiastic, frustrated, nonproductive, up against blank walls, we probably are not living under God's guidance.

These are some of the discerning questions we can ask ourselves about our choices and actions in the exciting adventure of the new moral awareness in our lives.

One of the changes in the transformed self will be the new experience of suffering. Formerly, our suffering arose mainly from our inner conflicts, fragmentations, and unhealed hurts. But as the inner healing grows, the suffering changes its nature. We begin to hurt for others. We grow into sensitive awareness of the suffering of others, not only of the people we know but also of the ones we don't. It begins to hurt to read or hear the world news. It hurts to see lonely, wrecked human beings on the street or in the bus stations. It hurts to see a neglected child, an uncherished old person, a man or a woman out of work or with dignity demeaned in any way. It hurts to see a suffering animal or a thirsty, withered plant.

We wonder where all this pain comes from, and we slowly realize that *it is God's pain through us!* As our relationship with God grows, we tune in more deeply to the pain God experiences when seeing and sharing the suffering we inflict on one another in this world.

But as our sensitivity and suffering grow, so must our roots in God's life deepen or we will be shattered. Yes, we were meant to become more sensitively and empathetically aware of others, but we were never meant to bear all that pain on our own shoulders, our own spirits. If we attempt to bear this pain alone (and many loving people attempt it), we will become exhausted, sick, and heartbroken. Eventually we will burn out or break down. It is an old and tragic story: many of the world's reformers and lovers have forgotten that they are human and not God; they have attempted to bear the pain and burden alone and either have been shattered or have hardened and become manipulators and assaulters of other people.

But if the new experience of pain for others is put into God's hands for transforming guidance, new empowered gifts will surface by which we can reach out to others in their suffering. Do not fear that God will allow you to become merely a helpless spectator of the world's pain. Powers of sharing, hearing, healing, relieving, releasing, and building will be given as your life goes deeper and deeper into God's life.

Fourteen years ago, a little girl we knew cried over the pain of animals. She told us that the next time she went to church, she asked God to turn her into someone who could help the world's pain. She did not know how that could be done, because she was very shy and timid. But today she is a loving, compassionate psychologist and the director of a mental therapy home, reaching out with healing powers to the sick in heart and mind.

A young boy we knew wanted to spend his life sharing the good news of the transforming love of God. But he was so terrified of speaking in public that the first time he knew he had to make a five-minute speech, he lost five pounds in one week and could hardly sleep. Now he is a preacher of tremendous, loving power, and his words and books reach the hearts of thousands.

A housewife, moved and sickened by the widespread hunger in the world, asked God to use her pain and her new awareness. Within a few years she has become a strong political force in her church and her community, working with released power in joy and pain to alleviate the injustice and cruelty of hunger.

Our deepening pain for others, offered to God, rooted in prayer, and increasingly dependent on Christ's strength, can and will be transformed and released by God into almost unimaginable gifts of love. Do not fear that the prayers of deep inner healing will turn us into passive, complacent jellyfish. We become the new creation, and the adventure is just beginning!

Gently, mercifully, with compassion for our timing and our type, God works within us with inexorable power, bringing forth that new creation of the fully alive human being. We are in the most merciful and the most skilled hands in the universe.

The healing of our powers will produce not only the compassion of love but also the passion of love. As we are healed, we will laugh as well as weep. We run, dance, fly, create and re-create, released by God in all our powers. We were created by God to be God's full children, heirs, and partners. When we have achieved a certain height, we will be called higher. When we have released a certain gifted power, we will be given a greater power. When we (metaphorically) learn to ride a wild horse, we will be given wilder ones to ride.

When God looks on us with radiant joy and says, "Well done . . . enter the kingdom," it certainly is *not* an invitation to aimless floating on fleecy clouds for all eternity. The kingdom was the metaphor for the ultimate redemptive power in the universe. We are being invited in to thrones and dominions of incredibly deepened power, responsibility, healing energy, and creativity.

Persons moving into the healing depths with God already, in this life, begin to realize and experience the power of the gifts. How can we safely receive them? How can we use them boldly, without abuse and misuse?

First, receive them as gifts. They are not of our making; we have received them as endowments. We did not earn them. Rather, we are being released to them.

Second, let the inner healing deepen, keeping apace with the release of our powers, or our powers may become distorted and manipulative.

Third, know that these powers, without exception, are to be used for the "washing of feet," as channels for compassionate, incarnate love.

Fourth, know that God through Christ is the enabler, the grace giver, who weds and redeems the powers within us. When the spirit of Christ says to us, "Friend, go up higher" (Luke 14:10), we will be empowered to be more incarnationally involved with the world of pain, not as a bewildered victim or onlooker but as one who sees authentically and heals with authority in Christ's name. In Christ, to go higher means to go deeper.

When James and John asked Jesus to be allowed to sit at his right hand and left hand in his kingdom, he asked if they really knew what they were requesting. To enter into that power meant, by definition, to be able to drink fully the cup of his suffering involvement with the world (Matt. 20:20–22). To be in power over others in that kingdom meant, by definition, to be in full compassionate identification with others.

Do we *really* know what we ask when we ask for healing, when we ask for wholeness, when we ask for the full release of our gifts? I think not. Not yet. Not altogether. But we already begin to drink that cup, and we already begin dimly to see that the only ultimate throne has on it the Lamb, the Suffering Servant, who is in the very heart of God. And the adventure of the transformed self is to love and to channel the joy and the pain of that central heart.

CHAPTER TEN

Spiritual Help for Christian Leaders

I abide with you.
I rejoice with you.
I suffer with you.
I heal you.
I awaken you.
I transform you.
I transform through you.

This is God's voice speaking not only to the world but to every part of the world; not only to nations and communities but to every individual; not only to humanity but to every aspect of struggling, evolving creation.

A Christian leader is a person who feels called by God through Christ to expend his or her center life and strength channeling and manifesting this transforming love of God on the frontier where creation meets chaos.

You are a Christian leader *if you feel thus called*, whether you are in charge of the choir or in charge of the Conference. If you teach a class, work on the finance board, call on the sick, join an intercessory prayer group, work on problems of hunger and injustice, delegate at a conference, concern yourself with the poor, or prepare a worship service, you are a Christian leader.

The ordained minister expresses this calling through full-time professional work. But the lay person responding to the inner call through varying gifts is no less a Christian leader, sharing many of the same rewards and stresses.

Increasingly, my personal ministry is concerned with

the stresses that the Christian leader undergoes. My work takes me to many ministers' and lay leaders' conferences, and I meet many tired, drained men and women. As I pointed out earlier, we are definitely more aware of the leadership problems of fatigue and stress than we were in earlier generations. We hear a lot more talk about these problems, but many of us still feel bewildered about the ways to heal them.

The point of this book, of course, is to share the various alternative ways of praying by which we can receive God's healing and nurture. This book is concerned with the inner healing of *all* Christians, not just specific leaders. This chapter, however, is concerned with the *special* problems and stresses within the life of the Christian leader.

One of the main causes of leadership fatigue is our temptation to feel that it's all up to us. This is the problem of super-responsibility. We feel that God's kingdom stands or falls according to the extent of our willpower, our righteous efficiency, and our power to love and heal. Perhaps we have learned to delegate responsibility outwardly, but we have not learned it inwardly. We carry the burdens of all upon our hearts and never take an inner vacation. We overlook Jesus' challenge to be the branches of the vine (John 15:4–5) and try to become the vine ourselves. Without realizing what has happened, we are trying to become the generators rather than the transmitters of the divine energy.

Even prayer itself can become exhausting if we approach it as an activity willed by us and initiated by us rather than as a response to the God who has already loved us forever and who holds us even when we turn away from prayer.

One major aspect of super-responsibility is the difficulty we feel in letting others serve us and minister to us. For so long, we have thought of ourselves as the nurturing ones, the loving, giving, strong ones, that it is a real struggle with our guilt to let our selves be helped and served by others.

There are many symptoms of deep fatigue, and sometimes they are confusing. Fatigue does not always show itself as outright tiredness. It can be manifested as anxiety and nervousness, restlessness, absentmindedness, clumsiness, annoyance over trifles, lethargy, unresponsiveness, apathy, exasperation at other people, a feeling of being driven or hemmed in, odd aches and pains, chronic or repetitive, small undiagnosed illnesses, unrestful sleep, loss of joy, compulsive eating or drinking, loss of appetite, compulsive reading, or procrastination.

If you are experiencing some of these symptoms and no physical cause is found, you should take a long, thoughtful look at your life and your attitudes. You may be in a state of serious inner fatigue.

You might ask yourself some pointed questions: Am I trying to be the source and resource for everybody? Have I begun to look on myself, rather than on God, as the limitless fountain of loving activity? Have I allowed others to look on me that way? Do I feel as if I'm never quite measuring up to my expectations for myself? Do I feel if I don't see to it, everything is going to collapse? Have I learned to say no sometimes? Have I been overdoing anything, such as counseling, meditations, intercessory prayer? Have I been pushing myself into certain responses, patterns of behavior, methodologies, and timing that are not really right for me?

For years, as a young pastor, I tried to be the super-organizer, the one who had no limits, the one who was the reconciler for others. Without realizing what I was doing, I was trying to become the vine, the source, rather than the branch. I was puzzled at my frequent annoying colds. Of course, my body and spirit were trying to make me "lie down in green pastures" for a little while. Our bodies constantly give us signals if we learn to listen to them.

Slowly and reluctantly I learned that only God is God. Only God is the endless source of regenerating love. I began to allow myself to be human, to have limits, to take some sabbath seasons for myself, to say no sometimes, to do some recreational things without guilt or worry that I was being selfish. I found it helpful to have little sabbaths during the day: a few moments each hour or two when I would put aside work, stretch, look out the window at something beautiful, lie on my back and listen to a record, breathe deeply, read a chapter of an amusing book.

If you suspect that you are deeply enmeshed in fatigue, it is wise to move into different forms of prayer for a while. You may need to lay aside for several days your intercessions, your deep searching meditations, and relate to God through some form of restorative prayer such as the ones suggested in chapter two. (If you are concerned or worried about laying aside intercessions, you can make the symbolic gesture of laying your intercessory list under a cross or next to a window in the sunshine as a sign that you release those dear ones to God while you take the replenishment you need.)

Sometimes a refreshing form of prayer is a parable walk. Take a stroll and ask God to show you through the activity of plants, insects, birds, animals, wind, and sun some special story, sign, or signal. I have learned some fascinating things about myself, God, life, inner growth through these walks.

Sometimes in our fatigue we ask to be ministered to and nurtured by music, a flower, fresh air, laying our hands upon a tree or shrub. And this is a real and deep form of prayer.

As we grow in our relationship with God, we learn it is not only preventive medicine to turn regularly to the nurturing sources but also an essential part of the relationship itself. God the vine, God the initiator, God the shepherd, longs to share life with us as part of our bonding, our connectedness, our mutual love and companionship, not just because we will break down and burn out without it.

Of course, to enter into that relationship *is* the heart of our prayer, the heart of our ministry, and it is the main source of our renewal.

Another main problem and stress in Christian leadership can be unawareness of inner wounds, hurts, or loneliness. This was discussed thoroughly in chapters three through six as a general problem for all of us. But it seems to be especially true of the minister or the leader. As with the problem of fatigue, we have thought of ourselves for so long as being the comforter of others that we forget we too have painful memories that need healing, deep inner fears and angers that need compassionate encounter.

One minister shared with me that though he had been working in counseling for years, and often led others in the healing of memories, he had not yet taken time to sit down and deliberately face his own deeply vulnerable, hidden, central wounded child. He was startled when he discovered it was there and had apparently been there all his life, feeling left out, different from others, inferior, and lonely. His leadership gifts and his counseling ability had covered up that little boy inside and had not encountered or healed it.

As he began to pray the prayer for the wounded memories and the deep, wounded inner child for *himself,* he began to notice many things about himself that he had formerly overlooked: his instinctive inner withdrawal and fear when challenged; a deep, competitive, someday-I'll-show-them feeling; an inner hopelessness that people could ever really like him if they ever really knew him. He actually hadn't realized that these feelings were still there, because he so quickly brushed past them in his ministry to others.

Unlike fatigue, this lack of awareness of the self often has no symptoms. You can suspect or diagnose this problem when you realize that for a long period of time, you have felt little or nothing at all inside. If you have experienced a condition of light general anesthesia over a period of months and years, you may well ask yourself if there is some inner pain you don't want to look at.

Sometimes this numbness will break down, and you spill over with anger, tears, or anxiety at periodic intervals, and then you pull yourself together and return to your numbness. Sometimes compulsive needs that seem to be growing are signs of inner neglected pain or unexplained anxieties that seem to be chronic.

If you suspect that you are neglecting unhealed areas

within, it helps to make a fairly regular practice of suddenly asking yourself at various moments through the day: "Just how am I feeling right now? Do I feel uncomfortable? Left out? Ignored? Conspicuous? Threatened in any way? Do I feel like a target? Am I feeling some necessity to defy or placate? Am I feeling at ease and relaxed?" This sudden honest question, silently directed inward, can be extremely helpful in learning to become aware of what is happening within yourself.

If you become aware of surprising feelings through this illuminating exercise, if you become aware that there are ignored hurts, angers, or grief, it would be well to turn to forms of prayer that cooperate with God's inner healing, such as the ones discussed in this book.

Another special stress for spiritual leaders is the sensitive pain felt on behalf of others. This was touched upon in the preceding chapter, with the warning that as the sensitive awareness for others increases, so should the roots of dependence on God go deeper.

One young woman minister shared with me her increasing difficulty in visiting a parishioner in the hospital. He was both paralyzed and afflicted with a skin disease. Though in constant pain from his skin, he could not move to ease himself. He just lay there with tears in his eyes. She found it harder and harder to go to him, each time she felt more broken and helpless. She felt shattered at every visit.

Many of us remember the pain of visiting a home where someone has just died. Many of us know the helplessness of watching someone going through the agony of divorce, the desperation of addiction, the hell of insanity. How can we confront it, share it, alleviate it without breaking under it?

It is just this point of our human weakness that is meant to be the doorway to our greatest strength. Where our rope ends, God's greatest sustaining power begins. No, we cannot go through those doors of pain in our own strength. We cannot wait to evoke the correct feelings, nor do we have time to sit down and work out a theological analysis of our approach. At times like these, we throw our full weight upon the living Christ and pray: "Living and loving One, I am just not up to this! It's too much for me. Take over. Take over all the way! Go ahead of me into that room and fill it with your light and healing. Then when I get there, speak through me, act through me, touch through me."

The response to this prayer of utter dependence is perhaps the greatest miracle of all. We are surrounded by an immensity of power and love that is almost indescribable. We know that we are not alone in that room and that what happens through us is not coming from our own little willpower or power to love. Once we have experienced this in a shepherding role, we never forget it.

Another great stress, often overlooked or even unknown, is that of being drained by others. It is easy to recognize overt signs of dependence from others. We can usually spot such signs when others constantly visit, phone, write, imitate, or ask us in one way or another to take over their responsibilities of decision. It is much harder to identify when we *internalize* the problems and symptoms of the persons we are trying to help. We may not be consciously thinking and worrying about them, but perhaps we begin to feel within ourselves their fear, anxiety, and anger. Perhaps we begin to dream restlessly at night about them. Perhaps we feel some physical symptom or stress that is not natural to us.

A more subtle draining experience occurs when persons, desperate for light and nurture, draw directly upon the energy field of the nearest leader. This is usually an unconscious process. The persons draining us usually do not know what they are doing, and they intend no harm. By not knowing how to take needed strength from God or from the sea of living energy around them, these persons draw it from another individual. Most Christian leaders, especially those in work of deep personal encounter, are familiar with the sudden onset of cold, dizziness, inexplicable anxiousness or irritability, sudden exhaustion. The difference between this experience and that of chronic fatigue due to our own overwork and conflicts is the suddenness of its onset in certain situations and its unrelatedness to our usual reactions to people and places. It seems to come on us like a draining force from outside us.

It may be somewhat similar to Jesus' experience when the hemorrhaging woman quietly touched his garments for healing: "Jesus, perceiving in himself that power had gone forth from him, immediately turned about in the crowd, and said, 'Who touched my garments?'" (Mark 5:30). Something seems suddenly to be taken from us.

If you suspect that you are either internalizing someone else's problems or being drained by someone else's need, you might ask yourself these questions: "Do these feelings of sudden fatigue, cold, dizziness, anxiety, irritability, weakness seem to come in certain counseling situations or in certain groups or relationships? Is there any special group or person with whom I feel unwell or uneasy? Has there been any change in health, energy level, since I began meeting with that group or that person?"

It may not always be possible to identify the persons who have this effect on us. However, if we become aware that we feel unusually beset or exhausted in certain situations, we would be wise to take seriously Paul's words about the "whole armor of God" (Eph. 6:11–20). He means there are places and times when we need spiritual protection. He does not necessarily mean that we are being assaulted by evil forces at these times. Most of the time, it is probably a need to protect ourselves from undue fatigue, but it may be the source of many unexplained illnesses and stresses. This is a surprisingly neglected concern among Christian leaders who are usually the first victims. The scriptures are full of warnings about the need for spiritual protection, and God's power is often referred to as the fortress, the strong pavilion, the shield, the rock, the high mountain, the sheltering wings.

Christian love releases us to full encounter and involvement with other people. Certainly we don't want to return to our old defensiveness and withdrawals. How can we claim spiritual protection and maintain at the same time bold and compassionate relating?

We can claim the light and life of the risen Christ as the enabling and effective strength in our situation. This can be done by the soaking prayer discussed in chapter two in which we visualize ourselves completely clothed in the radiant light of Christ. It does not need to be a long prayer. Even in the *midst* of the sudden draining situation we can silently pray:

> *In the name, by the power, and through the word of the living Christ, I claim the cloak of light for my protection, and I place myself and all those with me under Christ's light and guidance. Christ is the only source of power and nurture in this room, and it flows to all who need it.*

With such a prayer, we are not walling ourselves off from others. Rather, we are enabled to move even closer to others, because it is now no longer our own energy field that is being tapped. The limitless energy of Christ has taken over the situation. Usually we feel an almost instant renewal of warmth, peace, and strength.

As indicated earlier, this is not some magic power we manipulate. God's protecting love already forever embraces us. The only thing that has changed is our willingness and conscious decision to claim and internalize and make manifest the enabling power of Jesus Christ.

One stress that is a special burden to Christian leaders is the temptation to equate ourselves with our work. It is so easy to identify ourselves with our work, judging our self-worth only by results. We demand closure. We expect immediately apparent fruitfulness, and if success is not apparent, we feel diminished, judged, and unworthy.

One of the greatest signs of spiritual growth is the emerging willingness to release results into the hands of

God. To be open-ended, to be able to accept temporary ambiguity and postponement, is a manifestation of the trusted relationship between the self and God.

The great Japanese Christian pastor and social reformer, Toyohiko Kagawa, was stalled midway in his life of incredible activity as head of the social welfare bureau during the worst of the depression in Japan in the 1930s. He was ill in bed for months. Friends who went to see him thought he would be wild in his restlessness to get back to work, knowing how badly he was needed. But Kagawa reportedly told them: "Work is not the purpose of my life. I am giving life that I may live. My life is focused in this one moment. My present task here and now is to be in fellowship with God." I have always remembered Kagawa's witness when I have been blocked in my work or forced to accept postponement in results. Our work, our task, is not the same as our identity.

Indeed, perhaps the ultimate spiritual help to all Christian leaders lies in Kagawa's challenge: "My present task here and now is to be in fellowship with God." This is the meaning of our work. This is the meaning of our praying.

My dear friends, we are now God's children, but it is not yet clear what we shall become. But we know that when Christ appears, we shall be like him, because we shall see him as he really is.

—1 John 3:2, TEV

This is the grace, and this the growth. We are already God's children, no matter how immature we are, no matter how fragmented we are. Ahead lies the promise that as we grow in God, we shall increasingly see and unite with the Beloved and become more like the Beloved.

Held in that embrace, healed in that compassion, made whole, and released in that deepening relationship, all that we are will be continually reborn to new expressions of God's mysteries.

What shall that be like? We don't know yet, any more than the acorn knows what it will be like to be the oak. It does not matter. The only thing that matters is wherever we go, wherever we grow, God undergirds us, God goes with us, God goes ahead of us, God will be there to welcome us!

Flora Slosson Wuellner is adjunct faculty at the Pacific School of Religion in Berkeley, California. She received her B.D. degree from Chicago Theological Seminary and is an ordained minister in the United Church of Christ. She served as Parish Pastor in Wyoming, Idaho, and Chicago, Illinois. Rev. Wuellner has been an ecumenical retreat leader for fifteen years.

Among her several previous books are *To Pray and To Grow*, *Release for Trapped Christians*, and *On the Road to Spiritual Wholeness*.

Rev. Wuellner and her husband are the parents of three daughters.